ULTIMATE BASS FISHING LIBRARY

FISHING BASS COVER AND STRUCTURE

FINDING AND CATCHING BASS
WHERE THEY HIDE,
FROM TOP TO BOTTOM

MONTGOMERY, ALABAMA

INTRODUCTION

STRUCTURE VS. COVER

Bass are object freaks. In most waters, most of the time, you'll find them hanging somewhere close to an object of some sort. That object can be as inconspicuous as a lone twig rising 6 inches above the surface of a farm pond, or as imposing as a canyon wall towering hundreds of feet above (and below) the surface of a Western impoundment.

Some anglers use the term, "structure," as all-inclusive. Over the years, however, Bassmasters have come to distinguish structure (any change in bottom contour) from cover (man-made or natural objects attached to the bottom). Whatever the terminology, structure and cover provide invaluable habitat for black bass.

Bass use various types of structure and cover depending on the season, the type of water and other environmental factors. The first step in patterning bass, therefore, is learning their preferences in each set of conditions. Sorting through the myriad options can be a dicey proposition.

Take rocks, for example. Rocks come in different sizes, shapes and composition. And in many cases, only certain types of rocks will attract fish during specific times of the year. During prespawn, bigger is better, since large, flat rocks baking in the sunshine of a late winter afternoon radiate warmth into the surrounding water. During the spawn, pea gravel becomes the rock of choice among bass making spawning beds. In postspawn and into summer, tapering rocky points and sheer bluff banks emerge as the favored geology.

Other classes of cover offer plenty of alternatives as well, including standing timber and laydowns (wood), hydrilla and peppergrass (vegetation), and ridges and dropoffs (structure). And while cover structure can be easy to find, a bass fisherman must be familiar with all kinds in order to spend a successful and enjoyable day on the lake.

This book is a complete guide to cover and structure: where to find it, how to fish it and when certain types are most productive during a given season. All of the bases are covered, from locating and fishing structure in massive impoundments to cover endemic to small streams and tidal rivers. In each case, the connection is made between the objects and the best lures and presentations to maximize success.

Cover and structure. They provide the fundamental connection between you and the fish. Learn more about them in the pages that follow, and you will become a more successful angler.

Copyright 2003 by BASS

Published in 2003 by BASS
5845 Carmichael Road
Montgomery, AL 36117

Editor In Chief:
Dave Precht

Editor:
James Hall

Managing Editor:
Craig Lamb

Editorial Assistant:
Althea Goodyear

Art Director:
Rick Reed

Designers:
Laurie Willis, Leah Cochrane,
Bill Gantt, Nancy Lavender

Illustrators:
Chris Armstrong, Shannon Barnes,
Lenny McPherson

Photography Manager:
Gerald Crawford

Contributing Writers:
Wade Bourne, Paul Cañada,
David Hart, Mark Hicks, Bruce Ingram,
Michael Jones, Frank McKane Jr.,
Bob McNally, Robert Montgomery,
Steve Price, Louie Stout, Tim Tucker,
Don Wirth

Contributing Photographers:
Charles Beck, Wade Bourne,
Paul Cañada, Soc Clay,
Gerald Crawford, Tom Evans,
James Hall, David Hart,
Bryan Hendricks, Mark Hicks,
Bruce Ingram, Michael Jones,
Craig Lamb, Bill Lindner,
Peter Mathiesen, Frank McKane Jr.,
Bob McNally, Robert Montgomery,
Dave Precht, Steve Price, David J. Sams,
Louie Stout, Gary Tramontina,
Tim Tucker, Don Wirth

Copy Editors:
Laura Harris, Debbie Salter

Manufacturing Manager:
Bill Holmes

Marketing:
Betsy B. Peters

**Vice President &
General Manager, BASS:**
Dean Kessel

Printed on American paper by
RR Donnelley

ISBN 1-890280-03-8

WHETHER MAN-MADE OR naturally occurring, cover and structure is the single most important key to unlocking the secrets of catching bass.

CONTENTS

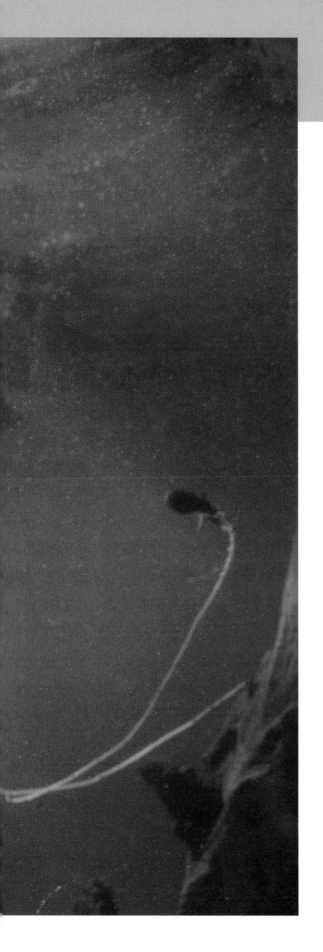

SEASONAL HABITATS

Knowledge of seasonal transition
periods is a key to unlocking
bass behavior . . .

SAVVY ANGLERS target a lake at its seasonal peak to maximize their chances of success.

SCHEDULE YOUR SEASON
Being in the right place at the right time is as important in fishing as it is in other sports, business and romance

ANGLERS WHO TAKE their fishing seriously — who expect and demand optimum results — prepare their bassing trips like a football coach boning up for a big opponent. They work on timing and perfect athletic execution to pick apart their adversary, targeting his weaknesses and taking advantage of every deficiency.

But unlike athletics, bass fishermen have the luxury of choosing their playing field. Bass may

always have the home field advantage, but anglers can time their trips when the home team is the most vulnerable. In this respect, choosing when to fish a lake, pond, river or stream is like the long-experienced football coach who lines up an opponent schedule so adroitly that when he finally plays his toughest adversaries, his own team is so confident, functioning so perfectly as a well-timed unit, that they play beyond their

individual abilities, and win in stunning fashion.

Every bass angler has a favorite lake or river, pond or stream. But the very best anglers have a lot of favorite waters. They pick among those premier places according to the season of the year, air and water temperature, up or down "cycle" in the bass population, water condition, bait availability, and many other factors.

These are anglers who have learned from experience that their livewells are more crowded at day's end if they make sure that their choice lake or pond, river or stream is in peak condition long before they launch their boats. They know that *when* they fish a given hot spot means as much to their success as where and how they fish it. This is why so many consistently successful anglers have a fishing schedule. It is an angling calendar as bulletproof as modern man can make it. They spend their precious fishing time only on the very best waters, and only during optimum fishing conditions.

It takes a lot of years and plenty of time for anglers to learn when they should be fishing which waters. But this is something any bass fisherman can do almost anywhere in America. The key is to think about your bass fishing — about the lakes and rivers you fish, their current conditions, and about the prime times you've experienced good fishing in the past. Don't leave such experiences to memory. Record them in a fishing log. Some anglers jot down on-the-water notes, which prove invaluable over time.

Be sure to record the best bass lures on different lakes, because if a buzzbait was deadly in the lily pads this spring on "Big Bass Lake," it's a good bet it'll work next spring in the lake's pads, too.

A growing number of anglers, including tournament fishermen Ken Cook, Rob Kilby and Rick Clunn, record information about bass lakes and reservoirs in a computer. These are money-making references for tournament fishermen when they return to a lake for an event. By checking notes about water levels, water clarity, air and water temperature, time of year, where, when and how past bass were caught, etc., these anglers are well ahead in the bass catching game.

But you don't have to be that sophisticated. Start a fishing log in a notebook or even with a small tape recorder. Tournament fisherman Shaw Grigsby uses a tiny recorder to make lake/river bass fishing notes. You don't have to be elaborate in your note taking, but be as specific as possible. List the exact dates and times you fish a spot, where, when and how you caught bass, the water temperature, air temperature, wind direction, current conditions, water clarity and level, and whatever else seems important.

It's a good idea to make a sketch of a spot — say, a cove or a small, submerged structure or weedbed — that yielded bass for you.

In 10 minutes, you can record a lot of important information about a bass fishing place. Do that every time you fish a lake or river, and in a very short time you'll have a valuable aid to help work out a remarkably effective schedule for bass fishing.

SHAW GRIGSBY uses a tape recorder to document information about the details of a productive fishing area.

seasonal fishing areas are in the least likely places, such as streams and other small waters.

Well-known Florida bass angler Doug Hannon is one of the innovative anglers who journals pertinent details about his fishing hot spots. Hannon has used such recorded information for years in his fishing, and by referring to it frequently, it has helped him properly time his fishing trips.

"I've always kept a logbook, and I wouldn't turn loose of my logs for anything," says Hannon. "One of the hardest things is to start a logbook. It's like a good education — it's hard to see the value of it at first. But the farther you get with a logbook, the more it evolves into the most valuable source of information you have."

Another plus for keeping a bass fishing log, is it helps determine when fishing is peaking at other nearby lakes or rivers you may not know well.

For example, by checking fishing notes, you may learn that bass in a large reservoir are in shallows, looking for spawning flats in April. Prime conditions are warm, overcast weather, stable water levels and a light, south wind. This knowledge can help time a spring bass trip to a similar reservoir 100 miles to the south — just

go a couple of weeks earlier than the prime time on your home reservoir.

Similarly, a clear, deep, spring fed lake farther north than the lake in your notes, should turn on for bass several weeks later.

Another important step in establishing a well-planned bass schedule is to obtain fishing advice and water condition information from lake or river areas. A great deal of such fishing information is available to all bass anglers, and they should actively use it in establishing seasonal bass fishing schedules.

Make friends with bait and tackle shop owners, with bass guides, fisheries department personnel, restaurant owners, newspaper outdoor writers, anyone who sees, hears or otherwise discovers what's going on in your favorite bass fishing region. These contacts greatly help in learning when to make a trip to a certain lake or river, and also when not to go.

A lot of bass anglers get into a fishing rut by only fishing one type of water, such as a large, clear reservoir or a big, deep river. To have a foolproof bass fishing schedule or calendar through the fishing seasons, an angler must have a wide variety of bass water available to him. Try to get a handle on large bass lakes and small ones; natural lakes and man-made waters; rivers, creeks, golf course ponds and borrow pits. Choose waters in as wide a geographic region as you can fish effectively, say a 200-mile radius of your home. If you're fortunate enough to live in an area that has several different bass species, that also can help you time trips to prime waters offering peak fishing.

Finally, never be shy about making a last minute change to your bassing schedule. You may be all set to head north for prespawn largemouth, but a sudden cold front that hits the night before the trip likely will send shallow water bass packing. A few late night phone calls, and a quick check of your logbook may help salvage your fishing time by changing directions — heading south, where the weather is warmer, water conditions more stable and bass eager to hit.

KEEP YOUR MIND open when planning a fishing trip. If the conditions dictate a change in plans, then try a different type of water.

Cash In On "Cycles"

Almost every dedicated bass fisherman can recall the rise and fall of a favorite reservoir, natural lake or river. Typically, a "hot" spot yields incredible catches of bass to almost everyone for a year or two or three, then it seems like the whole world of bass fishermen descends on the spot.

Next comes the bass crash. Fishing is poor for a long duration, and so, few anglers visit the place.

But remember, the "cycle" of hot bass action can come around again.

In central Florida, for instance, sprawling Lake Kissimmee and nearby West Lake Tohopekaliga are gemstone bass waters. But like many lakes, they're cyclical in terms of fishing success rates.

Fisheries biologists regularly control the cycle of bass fishing on Kissimmee and Toho, however, by periodically lowering the lake level to kill unwanted vegetation and revitalize the habitat. Planned drawdowns on lakes by fishery managers can work wonders, and they should be noted well by bassmen wanting to tap certain waters at the top of their bass productivity cycles.

During a typical drawdown, exposed lake bottom hardens, so it becomes better habitat for gamefish, as well as improves spawning sites for bass when the water level is raised. When the lake floods again, bass go on a feeding spree, and premier bass spawns result over the next several years. All this brings about an upswing in the bass cycle on a drawdown reservoir, so watch for it, and schedule your fishing season there appropriately.

Drought also can cause a natural lake or pond to drop to a very low level, which makes it a good bet for rejuvenation when the water returns to normal (as well as a choice spot when it's low, as bass are concentrated). Anglers should therefore plan to fish such lakes a year or two following a return to normal water levels, looking for a peak in the bass cycle that may result.

The point here is that anglers always should be aware of any drastic change to water level, weeds and any other man-made or natural factors of a lake or river. Such things can be key indicators of upticks in bass population cycles.

As in playing the stock market, you want to ride the rising crest of the wave, not its fall. So when hordes of anglers flock to a hot fishing spot, that may be a warning to look for greener bass pastures elsewhere. And when you're reminded of bass water that once had great fishing, it may be time to check the spot again.

FINDING BASS UNDER COVER

Too much cover and too little time! Heed this advice

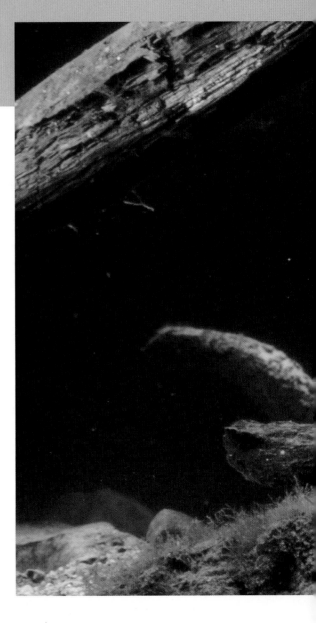

BEEN THERE, DONE THAT.
At one time or another, the average bass fisherman has encountered a situation in which there is so much cover that it's impossible to decipher where to go in the hunt for his quarry.

The encounter might be a lake full of standing timber, or one dominated by large hydrilla beds, that causes us to sweat. Or, maybe a fishing nightmare unfolds on an older reservoir, where hundreds of boat docks and boathouses serve as fish-holding cover.

The question remains, where does one begin? The first step is to determine which cover not to fish.

Three accomplished professional anglers share how they eliminate potential cover from a seemingly endless sea of opportunities. They offer timely tips for finding productive cover when fishing hydrilla, reeds, lily pads, standing timber and boat docks. Although each form of cover has its unique opportunities and challenges, a few principles apply to every situation. They provide the foundation for fine-tuning a productive pattern.

USE A CRANKBAIT when the bass are along the edges or inside grassbeds.

CUTTING THROUGH GRASS

Hydrilla and milfoil beds, similar to a flooded forest, are difficult for novice anglers to understand and fish successfully. Texas pro Richard McCarty approaches grassbeds the same way Ty Thomas analyzes timber: "When looking for fish in a grassbed, it still boils down to structure fishing," McCarty says. "You fish hydrilla as if it were structure, looking for the subtle points and depressions in the grass. That's where the concentrations of bass will be."

McCarty focuses on irregularities in grassbeds, especially along the inside and outside edges of the beds — depending on the seasonal pattern. He targets points, pockets, inside corners, ditches and depressions.

"Some bass are scattered throughout the grass," says McCarty, "but usually they gather on subtle points or in pockets in the grass. The pockets, depressions and irregularities along the edges reflect the changes in contours beneath the grass. It all relates back to structure."

The only way to determine where in a grassbed active bass are holding is to fish each type of hot spot. The location determines McCarty's choice of lures.

"There are two ways to fish the grass: along the edges, and in the grassbed itself," he says. "If I figure bass are on the deep, outside edge of grass, I use a crankbait or spinnerbait. If they're on top of the grass, then I use a topwater bait, spinnerbait or a lipless crankbait, which lets me cover water relatively fast."

McCarty recommends fishing the subtle structural changes thoroughly, because bass are often stacked on them. His favorite targets in summer are subtle depressions where the plants have matted over, creating a hidden pocket or tunnel. Sometimes these depressions and ditches may only have a depth change or 2 or 3 feet, but they frequently hold plenty of fish.

One key to refining a grassbed patterning is duplicating the presentation that triggered the first bite. It's important to note the characteristics of the cover where the bite occurred, he says. Be aware of the depth and thickness of the grassbed, and determine the structural feature that held the bass. Find that same combination of conditions elsewhere, and you're in business.

ELIMINATING UNPRODUCTIVE areas is the key to success on fisheries with an overabundance of cover.

READING REEDS AND PADS

Fellow Texan Clark Wendlandt has built a solid reputation through his skills in fishing lily pads and emergent vegetation, like reeds. He developed those skills during his guiding days on Gibbons Creek Reservoir near Houston. He approaches emergent vegetation and lily pads in a similar manner, beginning his search by looking for the depth and structural features that match the season.

The accomplished pro explains, "I always try to find reeds with a little bit of depth around them — around 3 to 5 feet. Most stands of reeds along the shoreline are in 1 or 2 feet of water. That's enough during spring and fall, when bass seek the warmer water of the shallows, but for most of the year, that water is too shallow. Lily pads are very similar to reeds in that aspect."

Lily pads are different from reeds in that — during spring especially — bass will swim well back beneath a lily pad field. During that time, Wendlandt fishes a variety of "search baits," making long casts and covering as much water as possible. In the thicker lily pad fields, the Texan uses a

BOAT DOCKS sometimes require methodical, precise lure presentations. Don't waste time on docks with low potential, advises Mark Davis.

RICK MCCARTY focuses on irregularities in grassbeds, especially along the inside and outside edges — depending on the seasonal pattern.

buzzbait or a rat, but if the pads are really sparse, he uses a soft jerkbait.

Wendlandt targets the sparser reeds and pads during the low light conditions of overcast days, when the bass' strike zone is larger. He enjoys best success in those conditions with spinnerbaits and soft jerkbaits, which trigger bites from fish cruising out in front of the cover.

On bright, sunny days or after a cold front, he recommends concentrating on the thicker pads or reeds, especially if there is deep water under the cover. Reeds and lily pads growing along points are often very good, if they're near relatively deep water.

One situation he loves to find is a stand of lily pads or reeds on a windward shore with baitfish working the edges.

Most of the year, Wendlandt likes to concentrate on the outer edges of both forms of aquatic vegetation.

"The best way to approach the cover is to get on a stretch that has several irregularities," he suggests. "I continue down the edge, flipping my bait into the most likely structure, whether it is a point, a pocket or an inner edge. When you get that first bite, observe where the bite came from and then try to repeat that presentation."

Other high-percentage areas are clearings inside the weeds where broken plants have formed a canopy over the opening. Likewise, plants broken or blown over, creating a mat in front of the reeds, provide excellent fish-holding cover. Wendlandt also recommends that anglers spend time fishing any ditches or drains that cut through a lily pad field or a stand of reeds.

Wendlandt, like the pros mentioned earlier, follows a systematic approach to eliminating potential cover. He considers the seasonal pattern and the current weather and water conditions in deciding which part of a lake to begin his search. Once he's in the appropriate area, it becomes a matter of fishing the irregularities in the cover.

Put another way, find the spots in cover that stand out from the rest, and you'll have outstanding success.

Dockside Matters

Arkansas BASS pro Mark Davis became somewhat of an expert on boat docks during his days as a guide on Lake Ouachita, a relatively deep, clear impoundment nestled in the foothills of the Ozark Mountains. Like many other top anglers, Davis targets boat docks that extend over structure that fits the seasonal patterns.

"In spring, I look for docks where fish are going to spawn," he notes. "The best spawning docks are in the shallower water of bays or in the backs of creeks, and they're built on pilings. Bass like to spawn next to pilings."

During postspawn, Davis switches his focus to docks and boathouses located at the mouths of creeks, along secondary points and where the creek channel swings near the dock. In summer and winter, the Arkansas pro looks for docks near relatively deep water and main lake structure. "You pattern dock-holding fish much like you would if the docks weren't there," he confirms.

Beginning in summer, especially on clear water reservoirs, bass tend to suspend off the bottom. Davis then switches from standing docks to deep, floating docks. "Bass like to suspend 5 to 15 feet beneath the floating docks," he says. "Floating docks are closer to the water, so they offer better shade and overhead protection. Because the fish are not related to the bottom, pilings become less important."

Finally, Davis recommends targeting older, wooden docks, which have well-established food chains and often hold better numbers of fish.

"I like to fish docks that look like anglers own them — chances are, the owners have sunk cover around the dock," he adds. "I look for clothesline or insulated wire tied to the dock, because that often means brush is suspended below the dock. The brush is for crappie, of course, but bass like it just as well."

The better docks will be closer to deep water. If a dock extends from shallow water to relatively deep water, it is more likely to hold bass throughout the day and as weather conditions change. Bass often choose positions beneath a dock that afford the best ambush points. For example, if current is present, expect fish to face the current and hold behind something that breaks the current. Davis recommends making multiple casts from various angles until a pattern is developed.

CONCENTRATE ON the thickest cover after a cold front, especially if there is deep water nearby.

THE FLOOR OF A LAKE is the foundation for feeding, spawning and other activities of bass.

BASS FISHING FROM THE BOTTOM UP

Bottom composition is the foundation of many bass catching patterns

AS HE IDLES OVER AN OFFSHORE SPOT, Shaw Grigsby carefully fine-tunes the gray line feature of his depthfinder and studies its liquid crystal display to get the answer to his questions.

With the first cast of the morning, David Fritts concentrates intently on the vibrations coming from his big lipped crankbait to determine something very important. Without a strike for the first 30 minutes in an unfamiliar area, Peter Thliveros precisely monitors the subtle movements of his Carolina rigged lizard in an attempt to learn more about the world below him.

(Opposite Page) SHORELINE GEOLOGY can provide clues about the lake's fundamental bottom composition.

The techniques these three top pro anglers employ may be different in form, but all are searching for the same type of information: bottom composition.

The makeup and hardness of the bottom are vital factors in the strategies of these and other expert anglers, but they are aspects of fishing that the average fisherman rarely considers.

"Bottom composition makes all the difference in the world," insists Fritts, former Bassmaster Classic champion and BASS Angler of the Year. "That is the first, most basic information you need to know when you start to fish a spot."

The floor of a lake is the center of much of the feeding, spawning and other activities of the bass. And the most successful anglers want to learn as much as possible about the bottom where they are fishing.

Whether they're fishing over or around a mud flat, chunk-rock bank, gravel shoreline, clay point, mucky ditch, sandy bar or limestone bluff, fishermen need to understand when and how the bottom is utilized by all species of bass.

"There are a lot of different bottoms," notes Fritts. "Sometimes the fish are on hard bottoms, and sometimes they're on soft bottoms. Sometimes they relate to hard spots — like a shellbed — on a soft bottom. Other times, they relate to sand, gravel or a specific type of rock. Or it may be a couple of different types of rocks together on the bottom.

"Even if my pattern is fishing wood, I want to know exactly what the bottom around it is like. That's how important I think bottom composition is."

THE TYPE of bottom — soft, hard or a combination of the two — will determine fish positioning even around boat docks.

Oklahoma pro Kenyon Hill also recognizes the importance of bottom composition.

"Not many people consider the bottom when they're fishing shallow cover like lay-downs, willow trees, boat docks and the like," notes Hill, a three time Classic qualifier. "But bottom composition plays as big a part in shallow water as it does in deep water."

When establishing a pattern, some pros go to great lengths to determine the exact size, shape and even color of rocks holding bass. Or they may target bare spots on a silt-laden ledge or grassy flat. Regardless of the situation, these guys try to learn as much about bottom composition as they can.

DECIPHERING THE BOTTOM

Today's easy-to-read liquid crystal depthfinders allow fishermen to get a good idea of the bottom composition before they ever make a cast.

"One of the neat things about my Lowrance unit is the gray line feature, which tells me whether the bottom is soft or hard," Grigsby says. "It really comes in handy in shallow water in spring when I'm hunting for spawning areas."

On his and other depthfinders, a wide black

line means the bottom is soft muck, which isn't the preferred spawning ground for bass. A thin line means a hard bottom — sand or gravel — where bass love to bed.

Some pros want to learn more about the bottom than a sonar's transducer can reveal.

In shallow water, Hill simply jabs his rod tip in the water to get a better idea of the firmness of the bottom. Beyond that depth, Thliveros relies on his advanced skill with a Carolina rig to tell him more about the floor.

The heavy sinker of the Carolina rig drags the bottom and tells the Florida pro whether he is fishing a hard or soft bottom, and it reveals the types of objects found on that piece of terrain.

Fritts is such a masterful crankbait fisherman that he can gain similar information through his diving baits. As the big diving bills of the baits drag the bottom, his experienced hands can differentiate between a hard bottom and a soft one, and they can indicate the presence of cover such as stumps, rocks and weeds.

SEASONAL IMPORTANCE

Every bass enthusiast worth his baitcaster knows that all species of bass prefer to spawn on a hard bottom. But few understand the other seasonal ramifications as they relate to bottom composition.

"In general, bass seem to prefer a hard bottom most of the year," Hill states. "There are exceptions, but if you can keep your boat over a good, solid bottom, your odds of catching fish will be better."

Color can make a difference as well. In early spring, dark bottom bays on the northwestern shores of a lake are the first to warm, attracting forage species, panfish and prespawn bass. The dark terrain retains heat better than a lighter floor.

"The northern shore of the lake receives the most direct impact of the sun's energy," says Ken Cook, a past Classic champion and fisheries biologist. "The muck on the bottom will absorb that energy and then transmit it back

EXPERTS LIKE **Kenyon Hill target firm bottom areas in the fall and winter.**

Bottom Facts

For most knowledgeable fishermen, the basic importance of bottom composition hinges on two things: whether it is suitable for spawning and which kinds of vegetation it will support. However, other bottom characteristics are helpful to know.

■ Alabama pro Tim Horton, a former guide on Pickwick, Wilson and Wheeler reservoirs, emphasizes that smallmouth bass prefer sandy pea gravel banks for spawning.

"Gravel is normally an area that bass use only for a limited amount of time during the spawn," adds Denny Brauer, a veteran Missouri pro. "The exception, and a favorite of mine, is pea gravel pockets next to chunk-rock banks. The gravel banks are at their best if they have some other type of cover to help hold the fish. On gravel banks, the bass love the bottom makeup, but they also like the security of some type of cover."

■ Boat ramps provide the ultimate hard, clean bottom, yet they rarely are fished, according to legendary angler Bill Dance. A ramp retains heat from the sunlight, promotes algae growth that attracts baitfish and provides a wide-open ambush lane for bass.

■ Small, baseball-size rocks make prime habitat for bass and their food chain. They provide hiding places for crawfish and other forage, as well as enough surface area to promote the growth of algae and moss.

■ Muddy bottoms are usually a poor choice for fishermen. One exception: A strong wind can create a mudline that attracts plankton, baitfish and panfish. The opportunistic bass will usually be positioned on the muddy edge of such lines.

■ Lily pads grow in soft or semisoft bottoms.

■ Limestone bluffs are more porous than many anglers realize. Most will have a variety of underwater holes that make great habitat for bass.

■ Dark-colored bottoms (like black shale) provide better concealment for marauding bass than does lighter terrain.

■ Sandy bottoms enhance the growth and variety of aquatic vegetation.

■ Maidencane, a universal reedy vegetation, grows on firm soil.

■ Shellbeds can be a gold mine for fishermen. "A lot of open water fishing is centered around shellbeds left behind by mussels," Thliveros says. "I grew up fishing the shellbeds in the St. Johns River, and I look for them everywhere I go."

more directly into the water. So this is where you find the early prespawn bass.

"In spring, the spawning urge becomes a major factor in developing patterns, so then you're looking for places where bass can find a good, hard substrate. They will seek out places where the harder bottom prevents their eggs from being covered by silt."

Silt and muck bottoms are poor habitat for spawning, but bass in some lakes will fan out beds in areas where the silt is not too thick. In lakes and reservoirs where hard bottom is not available, bass adapt by spawning on stumps, logs, angled tree trunks, the roots of aquatic plants and submerged debris, like discarded tires.

After the spawn, Thliveros has found that bass relate to soft bottoms, like red clay in lakes throughout the South. He theorizes that bass are drawn to these bottoms because they are a preferred spawning habitat for shad.

In the summertime, Fritts points out that bass utilize a variety of bottom types, especially red mud and clay areas. Most experts target firm bottom areas in the fall and winter.

TARGET THE TRANSITION AREAS

Bass anglers who understand the intricacies of fishing vegetation know that transition areas — where two or more types of grass mix — attract bass. The "edge" between two different types of bottoms can be just as productive, according to pro Denny Brauer.

"Soil changes are one of the subtle patterns I look for because they normally go unnoticed and unfished," he elaborates. "A few examples of what I look for are sheer rock turning to broken rock, gravel turning to sand and mud turning to clay. Any change or edge can hold fish. Check these spots. They only take a few seconds and can lead to some strong patterns. Just the color of the soil can be a preference for the fish."

The most successful of today's tournament pros have come to realize the importance of bottom composition. After all, it is the basic foundation for the watery habitat of all species of bass.

EMERGENT VEGETATION

Weeds, weeds everywhere —
that is the problem.
Here are the solutions . . .

HOW TO FISH EMERGENT VEGETATION

If your lakes have bulrushes, cattails and other emergent plants, you need to know how to haul bass out of them

THEY GROW LIKE SPECTATORS to a lake's timeless existence. They line its banks and sprout from its shallows. They sway to the rhythms of waves that roll across its open water. And they shelter and sustain its creatures: snakes, frogs, insects, crawfish and regular fish — especially bass.

They are the emergents: reeds, bulrushes, cattails and grasses. These water plants are found in lakes from south Florida into Canada and from the East Coast to West. They are more prevalent in natural lakes than in man-made impoundments. However and wherever they grow, when they coexist with bass, they are a preferred habitat for these fish, and anglers should learn to comb them.

Two qualified instructors in this endeavor are Larry Lazoen of Port Charlotte, Fla., and Dick Garlock of Alexandria Bay, N.Y. These experts live at opposite poles of this country's bass fishing spectrum: Deep South, Far North. Yet Lazoen and Garlock share amazingly similar views on the intricacies of fishing emergent vegetation.

EMERGENTS IN PRESPAWN

During the prespawn migration from deep water, most bass stage in the first ring of emergent vegetation they encounter as they migrate from deep water — usually deep reeds or maidencane.

"Before they move to their spawning areas in January, they'll hold along the edges of these deepest reeds or grasses.

(Opposite Page) LOOK FOR irregularities in vast spreads of emergent vegetation, where bass will position themselves to ambush prey.

USE A SPINNERBAIT to quickly cover water, and lock into a pattern for bass holding in emergent vegetation.

Emergents
North And South

The parallels between Garlock's New York strategies and Lazoen's Florida patterns are striking. Jigs and spinnerbaits are the main baits in both places. Spring and summer offer the best fishing, while in fall, bass in both regions leave emergent cover. Outside edges, holes, thick clumps and spawning flats are the hot spots in both Northern and Southern waters.

These parallels are no surprise. A bass is a bass is a bass, North, South, East, West or in between. If cover and food sources are similar, the fish will react similarly regardless of location. Only the timing may vary due to latitude and how soon the water warms up in spring.

This is why anglers all over the country can use Garlock's and Lazoen's methods to fish emergent vegetation in their home lakes. It doesn't matter where you are. What does matter is what you've got and how you handle it. Handle cattails, bulrushes and standing grass like these two anglers do, and you'll find yourself on the butt end of a bowed flipping rod more frequently than you have been.

LARRY LAZOEN switches to finesse baits after locating bass with a reaction lure. A focused, methodical presentation results in more fish, he says.

During this time, the fish are fairly easy to find. In my opinion, the prespawn offers one of the best chances of the year for both heavy catches and big fish."

During this period, Lazoen looks for points along the deep border of this vegetation. "These are little points or sags, such as any irregularity from a flat line of reeds or grass. I'll get my boat in next to the reeds and then look along the edge to see these spots."

Lazoen fishes his way from one of these places to the next, casting either a spinnerbait or a plastic crawfish across, beside and into the points and holes. Once Lazoen establishes a pattern, he slows down and works high potential reed and grass with a more thorough, conventional approach. When a strong prespawn migration is under way, Lazoen says anglers can catch bass off the same points or holes day after day. These spots are like mileposts for the movement to the shallows. New waves of fish are continuously swimming into the weed edges.

EMERGENTS DURING THE SPAWN

When spawning shifts into full swing, Lazoen concentrates on fishing what he terms the "outside of the inside." After motoring through the reeds and exiting this cover on the shallow side, he turns parallel to the reed line and begins casting back into the cover toward the center of the lake.

"Good spawning habitat is a combination of several conditions," he notes. "The water should be fairly clear. The bottom should be hard and clean, not mucky. Water depth should be from 1 to around 2 1/2 feet deep, and pencil reeds or flat lilies are usually the predominant vegetation."

KEY TO BASS LOCATIONS
1. Points of reeds; 2. "Bellies"; 3. Boat trails;
4. Inside edge of reed line; 5. Edge of shoreline
vegetation; 6. Thicker reed clumps; 7. pockets;
8. Outside schoolers

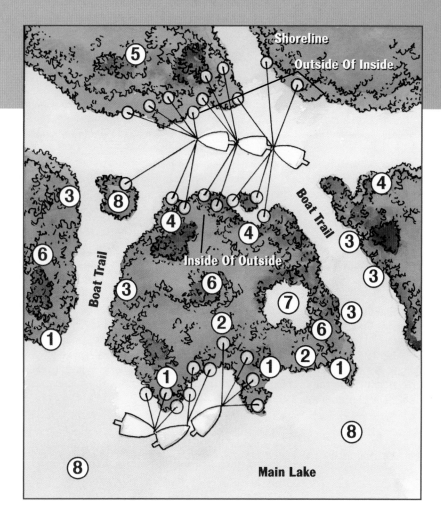

He finds these areas by idling along reed lines and watching for areas that meet these requirements. He says spawning beds will be clustered along the edge of the reeds and in small openings back in the reeds.

"I just move through bedding areas, staying back and casting as far as I can, then reeling as fast as I can. If I'm in a good spot, I'll pull the craw over two to five beds every cast. Chances are one of those fish is going to blow up on it instinctively."

EMERGENTS IN POSTSPAWN

"The postspawn is one of the hardest times to catch bass in emergent vegetation," Lazoen states. "Now they're stressed and sluggish, and they filter out through the cover and begin moving back toward deeper water. So the best approach for catching them is to hunt-and-peck. I get right in the middle of the reeds and

UNDERCUT BANK
Where cattails and other reeds grow in mucky bottom, holes washed out beneath reeds are bass magnets.

Emergents In Shallow, Natural Lakes

Florida's lakes have smooth bottoms instead of the irregular topography found in man-made reservoirs. So, bass in these shallow, natural lakes relate primarily to vegetation, which is the predominant structure. Included on this green list are the emergents: reeds, bulrushes, cattails and standing grasses also found on many natural lakes nationwide.

Lazoen says that bass set up in predictable patterns at various times of the year. The key to fishing success is in knowing when to fish which pattern, then finding the right spots and working them with productive baits and techniques.

Before considering Lazoen's seasonal patterns, anglers should have a basic understanding of how natural lakes in his neck of the woods are put together and how the vegetation relates.

The center of a lake is typically open and relatively shallow with a flat, featureless bottom. Some lakes may have bottom grasses, pondweeds and/or hydrilla growing in their deepest areas.

Moving from deep to shallow water, different types of vegetation characteristically grow in different depths and bottom content. In lakes with gentle slopes, plant species tend to grow separate from each other. In lakes with steeper slopes, species compatible to the same general range of depths and bottom types usually overlap.

Continuing toward the bank, the pencil reeds and flag lilies typically thin out into a shallow zone of open water between them and the bank, where cattails grow. These latter flat reeds can root in only a few inches of water or as deep as several feet. They normally sprout in mucky bottoms.

flip and pitch to any little hole or clump where a fish can hide."

Lazoen says the bass prefer certain reed flats over others, and they tend to scatter through the weeds instead of concentrating in one place. For this reason, he stays on the move and casts constantly. Best areas to try in the postspawn are where the reeds are thicker or growing in clumps. By summer, bass normally work their way back to the deep reed or grass edges, where they held in the prespawn. If the lake has hydrilla or other dense midlake vegetation, many fish will spread out into it. But if there is no midlake vegetation, most bass linger on the deepest reed line through the warmest months.

Lazoen says early and late in the day, summertime bass will be in open water next to the reeds or grass. To catch them during these periods, he casts spinnerbaits and lipless crankbaits parallel to the cover. If these baits don't produce, he changes to plastic worms or his inevitable Wacky Craw, which he casts or flips along the edge of the reeds.

During midday, the bass pull back into the reeds 2 to 3 feet, where the cover provides overhead shade. He moves tight to the cover and flips back into it.

CATTAILS IN NORTHERN LAKES

The bass fishing season in New York is closed until late spring, so Garlock's bulrush and cattail fishing efforts begin on opening day and run through summer. As in Florida, when fall starts, the fish abandon the emergents and head elsewhere.

"The main thing to look for is where a stand of cattails is undercut. In other words, say they grow from shore out into the water, but generally they're so dense the fish can't get back underneath them. Now, in areas exposed to wind, some places under the cattails' outer edge will be washed out. These are the very best places to fish this vegetation."

Cattail undercuts are favorite spawning sites. "At the beginning of our season, we catch a mix of smallmouth and largemouth from these spots. But the smallmouth don't use cattails as much as they do reeds, and those that do don't stay in them too long after spawning. A couple of weeks into the season, you don't catch anything but largemouth out of the cattails."

Garlock practices a simple method for fishing cattails. First, he finds likely areas by examining maps for shallows where these plants should grow. Then he visits the spot and studies the cattails. He idles along and looks until he finds the right combination of undercuts and water depth, and then begins fishing.

At the start of the season in upstate New York, bass feed mostly on snakes, Garlock believes, so he uses a jig with a plastic trailer. Later, they switch to frogs, and he changes to a jig-and-pork frog.

As he eases along the cattail line, Garlock drops his bait between stalks and into undercut holes. He actually jigs in the cover most of the time rather than along its front edge. "I like to drop my bait a foot or so back in and over a stalk so it'll fall straight down into the hole. I jig it up and down three or four times, then let it sit still for a second. If I don't get a bite, I'll pull it out and flip it into the next little hole," he says.

When bass are extra-active, Garlock switches to spinnerbaits and casts and retrieves parallel along the edge of the cattails. He positions his boat close to the cover.

"I'll cast down the line and pull my bait as close to the base of the cattails as I can," he explains. "I'll sort of slow roll it, lifting it and then letting it drop back down as I reel it in.

"Now, if a bass bumps the bait as it goes by but doesn't take it, I'll let it drop right back, and a lot of times it will hit again."

BULRUSHES ON NORTHERN LAKES

In Northern lakes, some bulrushes grow along the bank, but many sprout in deeper water away from the shore. Dick Garlock says bass tend to group in particular areas rather than disperse evenly through this cover.

"Smallmouth spawn in these deeper bulrushes, and if the water's clear, it's easy to find them. I just idle along and look for beds down in the reeds. I'll also watch for reeds that have round holes in them, like somebody took a cookie cutter and punched out some openings. Bedding bass in previous years formed these, and they're probably still good spawning areas."

Garlock says during and immediately after the spawn, he especially looks for reeds adjacent to shallow reefs and rockpiles. "Smallmouth stay back in these reeds during the middle of the day, and then move out to the rocks early and late to feed on crawfish. If I can catch fish off a couple of these rocky areas early in the morning, I know the nearest reeds will have bass in them during midday. Then I can go in there and fish these areas with confidence that I can catch something."

When fishing reeds, Garlock sticks with jigs with trailers and spinnerbaits, though now the order of importance is reversed. "I probably fish spinnerbaits more in the reeds. Normally, the broken reeds will be bent in one direction. I get on the side where the bent ones are pointing, and then I'll cast and pull my spinnerbait with the broken reeds instead of across them. This cuts down on hangups."

A LIFELIKE imitator, such as a frog, can elicit explosive strikes when fished along the edges of lily pads.

CATCHING BASS IN THEIR PADS
North, south, east or west, bass love lily pads

LILY PADS ARE LIKE GREEN PARASOLS, flattened out and floating on the water's surface. They effectively block out sunshine for bass lurking beneath them. Even on a hot, bright day, water under the pads remains cool and dark.

Bass feel comfortable and secure down in the pads' shadows. The pads' fibrous stems provide vertical cover that camouflages these fish and helps them ambush their own prey. They lurk back under the ceiling of vegetation and wait for minnows, frogs or other unsuspecting victims to happen along.

(Opposite Page) THE PRESENCE of baitfish is the common denominator to finding bass in the pads.

Not all lily pads hold bass, nor do the fish scatter randomly through those pad fields that do hold bass. As with other structure types, anglers must analyze lily pads to determine fish location and select baits and techniques most likely to catch them.

Alfred Williams of Jackson, Miss., and Nick Bowlus of Oronoco, Minn., are experts at catching bass from lily pads. Williams is a U.S. Postal Service employee who also fishes regularly on the CITGO Bassmaster Tournament Trail. His home lake is Ross Barnett Reservoir, which is filled with pads most of the year.

Lily pads are also common on northern natural lakes, and they're favorite hangouts for northern largemouth. Bowlus is an active member of the Minnesota BASS Federation and is active and successful on regional tournament circuits. He is recognized among his peers as one of the very best at jerking bass from the green dinner plates that dot Minnesota's prairie waters.

It isn't surprising that Williams' and Bowlus' choices of baits, tackle and methods for fishing lily pads are quite similar. What works down South, does likewise up North, and it'll work east, west or wherever anglers find a combination of this common aquatic cover and bass.

USE A Johnson Silver Minnow following a cold front. Allow the bait to flutter through openings in the pads to excite otherwise skittish fish.

WHICH PADS TO FISH?

To unknowing anglers, all lily pad fields look the same, and all appear to be bass havens. This leads to confusion and a tendency to simply start fishing any pads at

LILY PADS in close proximity to deep water are prime targets for bass.

(Opposite Page)
WHEN THERE is no evidence of feeding activity, go deep to find bass embedded in pads.

random. But Williams and Bowlus agree that this is a mistake.

Experience has taught these anglers that some pad fields are far more likely to hold bass than others. Two key factors determine a pad field's appeal to the fish. Anglers should store these keys in memory and then recall them when they begin their search for productive pad fields.

The first key is water depth.

"One of the main factors that determines whether a group of lily pads attracts bass is how near it is to deeper water," Williams begins. "So when I go to a new lake that's got lily pads, the first thing I do is start motoring around the pads to see where the deep water is. When I find some, I start by fishing the pads closest to the deeper area."

Bowlus says sometimes a minor difference in water depth beneath the pads can make a major difference in their attractiveness to bass. "In the lakes I fish, most pads have 1 to 3 feet of water under them. But a few have 3 to 4 feet, and these are invariably the best. I'm also always on the lookout for deeper pads."

The second key is the presence of baitfish. Bowlus is ever alert to the presence of baitfish. "I'll start through some lily pad fields with my electric motor, and I'll spook sunfish and see them dart away. But in other pads I won't see a single fish. If I start into a field of lily pads, and I don't see baitfish or some sign of feeding activity in 10 to 15 minutes, I'll go try someplace else. I do a lot of moving and looking until I do find pads that have baitfish, and then I slow down and fish them thoroughly."

TACKLE AND BAITS FOR PADS

Williams and Bowlus live hundreds of miles apart. Yet their specialty at fishing lily pads is a common bond, and not surprisingly, they use almost identical tackle and baits in this pursuit.

Williams opts for a 7 1/2-foot flipping stick fished on baitcasting tackle with 25-pound-test line. Up north, Bowlus goes with a 7-foot spinning rod and reel outfitted with 20-pound test.

In terms of baits for fishing lily pads, Williams and Bowlus use the same four basics: Snag Proof Frog; Johnson Silver Minnow weedless spoon, always with a plastic or pork chunk trailer; plastic worms; and jig-and-pigs.

Both anglers select lures to match the mood of the bass. Under cloudy, prefrontal skies, the fish normally hold just beneath the pads and feed actively. In this situation, Williams and Bowlus both rely on the frog and spoon. Also, Williams sometimes fishes a floating worm across the tops of the pads, while Bowlus frequently pulls his buzzbait over the vegetation.

When there is no obvious feeding activity — no bass busting or swirls or minnows skipping along the surface — the pad fishing experts switch to baits designed to go deep and slow — a weighted plastic worm for Williams, and a jig-and-pig for Bowlus.

TECHNIQUES FOR LILY PADS

When Alfred Williams has scouted the lily pad fields and found bottom structure he likes, when he's seen baitfish moving through the pads, when he's judged the activity level of the fish and

LILY PADS THAT BORDER A DROPOFF
To fish lily pads bordering a dropoff, position the boat over deep water and cast shallow with topwater frogs, spoons, floating worms, jigs or weighted worms. Keep moving and casting to different stretches of the lily pad edge until bass are found.

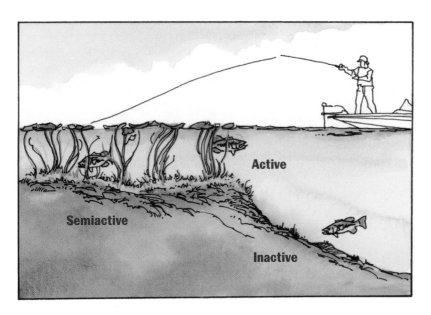

Active

Semiactive

Inactive

Additional Pad Fishing Tips

Alfred Williams and Nick Bowlus sometimes employ additional tricks and techniques to take lily pad bass.

"If I know a pad field is holding bass, but the pads are thick and I can't get to the fish, I may idle in there with my big motor and churn the lily pads and cut them up," Williams says. "Then I'll leave and come back four or five hours later, when things have settled down, and I'll have some good openings I can fish."

If bass are unusually spooky and Bowlus is flipping, he drops his jig on a pad adjacent to his target hole, and then he slides the bait off into the water.

"I try to make as quiet an entry as I can. If the fish are aggressive, noise doesn't matter much. But if they're spooky, I think a silent entry is a lot better than a loud one."

"If I can find a small, isolated pad field, I'll almost always fish it," Williams states. "A lot of times this means there's a shallow hump surrounded by deeper water, and this is prime structure."

Williams also pays special attention to logs, trees, brush, stumps and other features in lily pads. "These spots can be like magnets to bass. They're just that something extra to concentrate the fish. I always work them out thoroughly. The fish usually lay on their shady side," he says.

Both Williams and Bowlus use weedless props on their trolling motors, and neither one experiences significant problems in moving through pads. Bowlus has installed a weed cutter on his trolling motor, which helps prevent stems from wrapping around the prop.

decided which lure to use — only then does he get down to the serious business of catching.

"My approach to fishing lily pads is no different from fishing any other structure," he says. "People ask me how I fish lily pads. I tell them, 'The same way I fish a dropoff or a bank.' I just stay on the outside edge and look for the irregular spots, the pad points or corners, indentations or holes in the pads. Some bass may be scattered randomly through the pads, but more will be relating to these features."

Bowlus also starts on the outside. "I always fish parallel at least part way around a pad field before I move into it. I'm looking for the active biters that lie back under the edge of the pads watching for minnows. I'll use a spinnerbait or a buzzbait, and I work my way around, just like fishing a weedline.

"I pay special attention to anything that's different," Bowlus continues. "If there's a pocket just inside the pads, I'll cast to it with a spinnerbait. I'll let it flutter down in the hole, and then I'll pull it back out. And I especially like points. Sometimes points will hold fish when the little indentations won't."

Bowlus loves to crawl a Snag Proof Frog from one hole in the pads to the next. Once the bait moves into a new opening, he lets it rest motionless for a few seconds, and then he twitches it to trigger strikes from following bass. "One thing I do with the frog is to split the legs with a razor blade and stuff a small split shot in each one so they'll ride down in the water a little more," he notes. "But split shot or not, this is a superbait."

Williams and Bowlus like the Johnson spoon when the fish pass on the frog — when they're active in the pads but reluctant to strike on the surface.

"I can flutter the spoon down in the pockets, and they will hit it under water," Williams explains. He prefers black spoons and trailers in stained water and silver spoons with white trailers in clear water.

The technique with the spoon is simple enough: Cast it out and crank it back in. Bowlus says it's hard to pull the spoon too fast. "Sometimes, the faster I pull it, the more strikes I get," he notes.

When the spoon passes over a hole in the pads, both anglers stop the retrieve and allow the bait to sink a couple of feet. Oftentimes the fish will grab the spoon as it wobbles below the surface. "Usually they'll have it the instant they hit. There's no waiting to set the hook," Bowlus instructs.

If the mood of the fish is more passive, Williams changes to a "superfloater" worm (rigged weedless and weightless), and he slithers it over the pads. Again, there's nothing difficult here, just a straight pull with momentary pauses in holes. Strikes are usually ferocious, the fish inhaling the whole worm. "There's no waiting here. You just drop your rod tip, reel up slack and stick the fish," Williams says.

HOW TO FISH FLOATING COVER

Floating mats attract bass seemingly minutes after they form

THE PASSAGE OF THE COLD FRONT has produced a gully-washer, nearly 3 inches of rain in the course of the morning. Now water is rushing into the Missouri highland reservoir, carrying with it tons of sticks, leaves and other debris. In a matter of hours this flotsam will be blown into pockets along the shoreline, where it will jam up like a carpet on the surface.

In Minnesota, a thick line of dead grass blankets the shallows next to a rocky bank. In Louisiana, clumps of lily pads uprooted by a storm are blown into heaps that snag on cypress knees. From time to time, floating mats of vegetation, woody debris, man-made trash and other "materials" can be found on virtually all lakes across the country.

"Boy, I just love to fish these mats!" says 19 time BASS title holder Roland Martin. "They're not something you find every day, but when you do, they can be dynamite."

"Fishing mats has probably won me more money than all other techniques combined. I've had some tremendous, phenomenal days flipping this overhead cover," echoes Joe Thomas, another BASS tour veteran from Cincinnati. "This is one of the best methods ever for catching big bass,

A HEAVYWEIGHT JIG pitched to a point of floating vegetation is a productive means of catching bass.

yet it's one that's overlooked by a lot of fishermen, especially up North."

Martin and Thomas share many similarities in bassing preferences and style, but perhaps the greatest is their affinity for floating mats and debris. This is their mutual specialty; they describe the pattern in superlative terms.

OVERVIEW OF FLOATING MATS

"Mats are so good because they provide bass with two things they really like," Thomas explains. "First, mats offer a canopy of cover over their heads, and this gives them a tremendous amount of security. And second, the darkness beneath these mats creates an ambush window for bass. They can lie back in the shadows and watch for

food in the brighter adjacent water. It's the same as a mugger hiding in a doorway and waiting for a victim to walk by."

Martin and Thomas agree that floating mats may hold bass anytime, but each angler has his favorite set of conditions for fishing them.

"Absolutely the finest time to fish flotsam is when you have fairly cold water and a prespawn situation," Martin avows. "The typical situation is water rising after a big rain, and you may have a 5 or 6 degree temperature difference between the water near the surface and on down in the lake. Now this causes some real monster bass to come up out of deep water seeking this warmth, and they hide under the flotsam because of the cover it provides."

Thomas loves to fish floating mats under post-frontal conditions.

"These are great places to try after a cold front blows through and the sun's bright. These days are the toughest for most fishermen, but they're some of the best ones for what we're talking about. The high barometer and sun chase the fish back under the cover. But if you drop a jig down in front of them, they'll still bite it."

Martin and Thomas say that finding floating mats is a simple matter of covering water and looking for them. As a rule, though, certain areas are more likely to contain this structure than others.

"On highland lakes, it's common to find flotsam mats in little pockets along bluffs on the main channel or in short coves off channel bends," Martin

FOLLOWING A COLD front, bass will sometimes bury themselves in the densest floating cover before returning to the edges after the weather has stabilized.

THE WINDBLOWN side of an immense area of floating vegetation will position the fish on the leading edge, making them easier to pattern.

BASS WILL HOLD near a mat's outer edge or deep under the cover. Try both areas to determine what the fish prefer.

instructs. "Also, when a lake's rising, you can find flotsam in the backs and downwind sides of the coves."

Water depth beneath the mats is an important consideration. Depths range from very shallow to very deep, depending on the character of the lake and the location of the mat.

"If I'm fishing for bottom holding fish, actually working my jig off the bottom, then I don't want more than 8 feet of water under the mat," Thomas says. "Four feet is ideal, and I'd say you need at least 2 feet under a mat to consider fishing it."

"In a lot of highland lakes, you'll have these little guts that will have flotsam mats, and there will be 25 feet of water under them," Martin relates. "In this case, the bass usually suspend in the first 3 feet under the mat, and this is where you should concentrate your flipping. It's counterproductive to try to fish the bottom below mats over such deep water."

BASIC MAT FISHING TECHNIQUES

Far and away the best method for fishing mats is flipping. Martin and Thomas agree that this technique allows anglers to penetrate the overhead cover and deliver a bait to bass hiding below.

Tackle selection is ultimately important in flipping. The two pros use 7 1/2-foot, heavy action rods and 25- to 30-pound line. When it comes to baits, both anglers use jigs most of the time and plastic worms on occasion. Jig weight varies from 1/2 to 1 ounce depending on the thickness of the mat. Thomas estimates he fishes a jig 75 percent of the time.

Trailers on the jig vary between pork chunks and plastic crawfish. Martin sticks with pork if the mats are the primary pattern, and he is flipping. Most of the time when he is fishing crankbaits around other cover and only occasionally finding some flotsam to flip, he uses a plastic crawfish instead of pork, since plastic

Bring Out The Frogs

Although flipping is the method of choice for mats, Roland Martin and Joe Thomas both resort to one other primary tactic — pulling rubber frogs over this canopy cover.

"You wouldn't want to do this when the water temperature is 55," Martin explains. "But in summer, when the water is 80 degrees, pulling a frog over floating mats can be a killer deal."

"I use a Snag Proof Frog; it'll ride right over the junk without hanging up," Thomas says. "I fish it mostly early and late in the day. Or I cast it whenever I see movement in the cover — something that might be a bass chasing a minnow."

Thomas fan casts his frog across likely mats. "From any given boat position, I make the first cast along the edge of the mat, then the second cast into the mat at a 45 degree angle, and then the third cast at a 90 degree angle, way back over the cover. And I just repeat this, over and over as I work along or around the mats."

To retrieve the frog, Thomas holds his rod tip almost overhead, and he continually shakes the bait as he reels it in. "I fish the frog slower than most anglers," he notes. "I think it's a hard bait for the fish to home in on. If you fish it too fast, you're causing yourself some problems."

When he gets a strike, Thomas drops his rod and points the tip directly at the fish. Then he waits to feel pressure from the fish swimming with the frog before he sets the hook.

"Waiting does a couple of things," Thomas coaches. "First, a lot of times the fish miss the bait, and if you wait to feel them on, you don't pull it away from them. You can wait for it to float back to the surface, then shake it a couple more times, and the bass will usually come back and bust it again.

"Also, if the bass does get it the first time, waiting to set the hook lets it get a good bite on it and turn his head to swim with it, and this gives you a better angle to set the hook."

won't dry out like pork. Both anglers use big plastic worms for fishing beneath dense vegetation mats in warm weather.

Bass will hold either near a mat's outer edge or deep under the cover. The outer fish are normally more aggressive than those deep within. When fishing mats, an angler's first chore is to determine the location and mood of the fish. This means offering different options in terms of where the bait is presented.

"I usually ease up close to a mat with my trolling motor, and I start out by pitching to or flipping the edge to check for active fish," Thomas explains. "Then I'll get in a little closer and try 2 or 3 feet back in the cover, working my way along the edge of the mat. Mainly I concentrate on this 3-foot zone, since most of the active biters will be close to the edge."

Martin test fishes the edges too, but he also tries deeper in the mats, especially if some piece of vertical cover sticks through a mat. "If you've got a bush or stump or some reeds poking through the mat, a lot of times bass will hold beside them. Also, it's easier to drop a bait through a thick mat next to something vertical. There's usually a little hole right beside it, and if you flip your jig up there and work it around a little, it'll fall right through."

The actual flipping presentation for mats is simple, says Thomas.

"If the mat is over shallow water, I drop my jig right to the bottom. Then I lift it up very softly, feeling for a bass. I'd estimate that 90 percent of the strikes will occur on that initial drop. Most of the time you don't feel a thump or see movement in your line. Instead, there's just this spongy pressure, and if I feel this, I set the hook."

When fishing mats over deep water, Martin rarely allows his jig to drop more than 3 feet below the cover. "Again, in this case, the fish almost always hold right under the mat. So when my jig breaks through, I'm real careful with it. I stop it and jig it in the first 2 or 3 feet — that's the main area. Then I pull it out and try somewhere else."

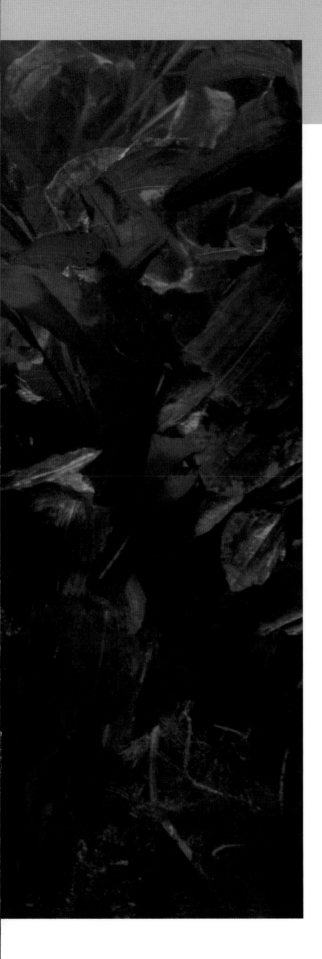

WEEDBEDS

The entire aquatic ecosystem
spends the summer here,
and so should you . . .

PINPOINT BASS IN WEEDBEDS
Find the sweet spots in vast weedbeds

ONE REASON why weedbeds are so good is they normally grow along a structure break, one of the prime attractants to bass.

PULL UP TO THAT big weedbed on your favorite lake, and you just know you're going to catch a fish. And why not? Bass hang around those weeds for one reason: to eat your favorite lure — or so you hope.

But be honest. Weedbeds don't always meet your expectations on your home lake, so the second-guessing begins. Did the fish leave? Are they inactive? What now?

Before you abandon a good area for the wrong reasons, consider other possibilities.

"If you've caught bass from a weedbed before, chances are good that it will continue to be productive," says four time Bassmaster Classic winner Rick Clunn. "However, each day can be different, so you must use a process of elimination to determine the pattern for that day."

In other words, you may have to fish the entire weedbed to determine the pattern for that moment, keeping in mind the pattern could change at any time during the day.

And don't overlook less obvious fish magnets that may be on the perimeter of the main weed patch, says Chip Harrison, a bass guide in Indiana and Florida.

"Some of the best sections of a weedbed can be right under the boat, and you'll miss them if you're not paying attention," he explains. "Fishermen can be so preoccupied with the visible 'edge' of the weedbed, they don't realize that some of the key elements are actually away from the main body."

The same can be said for the interior of the weedbed, adds Texas pro Alton Jones.

"Weeds tend to grow along a structure break, which is one of the reasons why they are so good," he explains. "However, everyone knows to fish the edge, so those areas get pounded. That's why I look for structures within the weedbed."

Jones examines weedbeds closely during the winter and spring when the weeds are sparse, watching for signs of stumps, logs, isolated boulders or even a change in bottom composition.

"Little pieces of hard structure or cover within a weedbed can really improve your chances of catching bass when they aren't out on the edges," he adds. "The structure is what makes the spot good; the weeds are a bonus that holds them more often."

You can get an image of the bottom beneath the weeds with a properly adjusted LCD fishfinder. Jones sets his dial in the manual mode and on the shallowest range, and then turns the sensitivity down until the weeds beneath the boat begin to fade from the screen. Soft bottoms appear black, while firm bottoms or hard spots will be grayer.

"The thicker the grayness, the harder the bottom, and the more likely the spot attracts bass," Jones adds.

Location is important, but you still need the proper lure presentation to get the fish to bite. If you only employ techniques that you prefer, you may be passing up a limit of good fish for a few dinks. Here are some proven methods from veteran weedbed anglers that can add new wrinkles to your own bag of tricks:

INTERIOR WEED TACTICS

• *Jig in a haystack* — When he knows the location of structure beneath massive weedbeds, Jones will push his way into the key areas and pitch jigs into the holes.

"I won a Texas tournament by fishing one little spot located 100 yards inside the weedbed," he describes. "All of the other contestants were fishing the outer edge."

His hot spot was a sandy hump he found during the early spring, before the weeds had grown to the surface. The hump was covered with schooling bass enjoying the security of the matted grass above them.

Jones says weighted worms would have worked, too, but jigs tend to catch bigger fish.

"Even though the weeds may mat on the surface, there are hollow areas down below," he explains. "Find a place where there

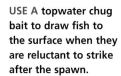

USE A topwater chug bait to draw fish to the surface when they are reluctant to strike after the spawn.

is a change in bottom structure and choose a weedless bait that can get to the bottom."

• *Postspawn poppers* — When bass are more reluctant to strike following the spawn, Harrison uses a Rebel Pop-R or Storm Chug Bug to draw them to the top. He keys on the shoreline (inside) edge of the weedbed, probing the cuts as well as the heavy weeds growing just beneath the surface.

"I normally work a surface chugger pretty fast, but not during the postspawn period," he explains. "I 'bloop' it two or three times and then pause it. The postspawn technique seems to be better when fished over weeds in dead-calm water."

• *Windblown pockets* — Windy summer days on clear lakes are tailor-made for spinnerbaits, says Harrison, especially on water that contains both largemouth and smallmouth.

"Windy days are my favorite for fishing spinnerbaits over weeds, because the fish usually are real aggressive," he explains. "It's ideal when the weeds come within 2 feet of the surface, regardless of the water depth."

Under those conditions, Harrison suggests fishing around the weedbed, covering both the deep edge and shallow side. His favorite spinnerbait is a 3/8-ounce tandem Nichols with gold blades and a blue iridescent skirt on sunny days and a chartreuse-and-white skirt under overcast skies.

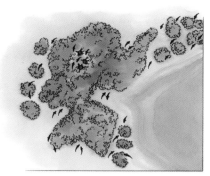

When fishing a weedbed, be aware that bass can be in several places — not just on the edge. Look for small, isolated clumps off the primary weedbed, and be alert for wood, rocks and other hard objects on the bottom beneath the weeds. Also, bass will use the irregular features in the weedline, such as points and inside turns.

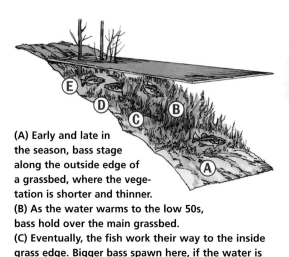

(A) Early and late in the season, bass stage along the outside edge of a grassbed, where the vegetation is shorter and thinner.
(B) As the water warms to the low 50s, bass hold over the main grassbed.
(C) Eventually, the fish work their way to the inside grass edge. Bigger bass spawn here, if the water is shallow enough.
(D & E) Before, during and after the spawn, bass prowl and feed along the inside grassline and around any timber or other cover present.

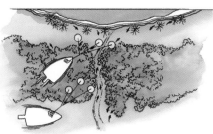

When bass are found between the bank and the inside grassline, position your boat over the grassbed and make long casts toward shore. When searching for bass along the outside edge of a grassbed, work parallel to the edge, casting at an angle to openings and other irregularities in the grassline.

"Target the pockets within the weedbed and use heavy line," he says. "The thick line adds buoyancy to the spinnerbait."

• *Bird dog tactic* — When Connecticut pro Terry Baksay is searching for bass in an area he's not familiar with, he relies on his "bird dog," a 6-inch bubblegum-colored soft jerkbait.

"I'm looking for any sign that a weedbed is holding fish, which will tell me to spend more time working it," Baksay explains. "The bubblegum Slug-Go is ideal because it draws fish out of the cover, even the ones that won't strike it. Once they follow it out to where I can see them, I know to experiment with other lures."

Once Baksay is assured the fish are using the weedbed, he'll switch to a piranha-colored Slug-Go or an alewife-colored, 5-inch Slug-Go Fin-S Shad that has a more ac-tive tail. He works the pockets and along the shallow edge of weeds, fishing both lures on or just below the surface.

"That's really effective during the early morning hours, when the water temperature is above 70 degrees," he adds. "It works in clear or stained water."

PROBING THE EDGES

• *Watch for "sweet spots"* — Pro Ken McIntosh isn't as interested in the weedbed as he is in the subtle changes along the bottom, where big bass hang out. That area where the bottom changes from hard to soft, or where the weeds stop growing, is the "sweet spot."

"I position my boat so that it's always on the edge, where there are no weeds," he says. "I make short casts and use the bait to try to figure out what's on the bottom. If I don't feel weeds, I guide the bait toward the weedbed. If it's clogging badly, I steer it away from the weeds."

When McIntosh locates a turn or point in the weeds, he slows down and works the area thoroughly with a Yamamoto spider grub, a jig-and-pig or a split shot finesse worm.

"Those little spots can hold a limit of fish," he adds.

• *Isolated clump patterns* — Weeds that grow in clumps away from the main weedbed get overlooked by most anglers, but not by the bass. On windy days, it's one of Greg Mangus' favorite patterns for fishing weedy flats.

"On windy days, the active fish may move away from the main weedbed and hold on small patches of grass on the windward side," he explains. "If the water is clear, I'll fan cast the area with spinnerbaits or soft plastic baits like tube jigs, spider grubs and lizards. If the water is stained and shallow, the Rat-L-Trap is good. Whatever lure I choose, I'll fish it fast, because I'm looking for active fish."

Texas pro Brian Schott "pumps" a 3/4-ounce Horizon's Ghost Minnow spinnerbait when searching for bass that use scattered patches of hydrilla located between a major weedbed and deep water. He says its deadly during prespawn or fall seasons when bass aren't in the chasing mood.

"The pumping action causes the bait to move erratically and triggers the reaction strike," he explains.

Schott winds the spinnerbait with a standard retrieve, but when it clips the weeds, he rips it free, causing the blades to twirl as the bait jumps from the weeds.

Main Lake Grassbeds

On large, grass filled reservoirs like Ray Roberts, Sam Rayburn and Toledo Bend, main lake grassbeds are consis-tent producers.

"The fish that spawn out on these main lake features don't typically do so until April," notes Texas pro Todd Fair-cloth. "The water out on the flats doesn't get warm enough until later."

Inside and outside edges play a major role in how bass position along main lake grassbeds. (The outside edge is the grassline closest to the main channel, while the inside edge lies on the side nearer the bank.) Throughout the stages of the spawn, bass follow these edges as they move to and from spawning grounds.

On reservoirs experiencing water fluctuations due to drought or annual drawdown, a well-defined edge typically forms between the bank and the grass-bed — as is the case on Sam Rayburn and Toledo Bend. But on Lake Fork, which has relatively stable water levels, you aren't likely to find a prominent in-side edge between the weedbed and the bank.

"The condition of our grass edges on Sam Rayburn Reservoir depends greatly on the water level of the lake," says Faircloth. "For example, the inside grass edge can be as deep as 12 feet or as shallow as 7 feet. No matter — the key to finding a concentration of bass is fishing the inside and outside edges."

Early on, bass hold along the outside grass edge. As water temperatures on these main lake flats consistently reach the high 50s, the bass move from the outside to the inside edge, then spread out over the ridge to spawn.

TRICKS FOR WEEDBED BASS

Fishing is a challenge when bass burrow deep in the vegetation

MAKE NO MISTAKE about it — lakes containing lush vegetation are fish factories and will produce better fishing days than most waters that are void of grass.

But there is a downside. Lakes with a lot of grass give bass more places to hide, and when they're not active, it becomes more difficult to present a lure in front of fish that are willing to strike.

"We all have our favorite ways of fishing around grass, but no single technique produces first-rate fishing all the time," says Michigan BASS pro Kim Stricker. While that may apply to fishing other types of cover, adds Stricker, it's especially true with bass around grassbeds.

"First of all, the bass can be anywhere — along the edges, burrowed up in the thickest clumps, suspended near the top or hugging the bottom," he explains. "The first thing you must do is figure out which section of the weeds the bass are using. Then you've got to choose a lure and presentation that matches the mood of the fish and how they're relating to that cover."

Anglers must take an open-minded approach when choosing lures and techniques, he adds, and should never leave a traditionally productive weedbed until probing it thoroughly.

Therefore, making one pass around a patch of weeds with your favorite lure probably isn't going to give you a true reading of what the fish are doing. And even if your technique is producing a few fish, another presentation may work even better.

While there aren't any secret lures for fishing weeds, several methods do seem better than others at getting less aggressive bass to bite. Here are some proven tricks employed by veteran weedbed anglers:

FINESSING CRANKBAITS

Many anglers dismiss the crankbait as an effective tool for fishing around vegetation because of the lure's tendency to snarl in the grass. That's a mistake, says Mark Davis.

"The crankbait often is my first choice for fishing weeds because it covers water quickly and helps me find the fish," says Davis, recognized as one of bass fishing's most consistent top performers. "I may switch to another lure that enables me to catch them better, but not until the crankbait helps me locate the fish."

Davis chooses a lure that runs just above the

grass and makes further adjustments by increasing or decreasing line sizes. For example, if the grass grows within 4 feet of the surface, he might use a crankbait that dives about 6 feet on 12-pound line, but runs shallower on heavier line.

"I'll have three crankbait rods on the deck, each with different sizes of line, so that I can fish the same lure at different depths over the top of the grass," he explains. "I'll start shallow and work deeper down the grassline until I determine just where the bass are staging in the grass."

Davis "finesses" the crankbait through the weeds under tough conditions, a method that works especially well in colder water.

"The common way to trigger strikes is to crank the lure down to where it's hitting weeds,

then stop momentarily and let it float away," he describes. "But I've found that by sweeping the rod — pulling against the lure slowly — I can get better control and sensitivity. I change the elevation of the

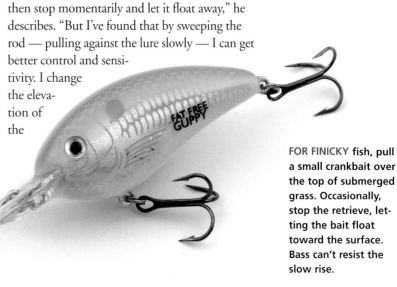

FOR FINICKY fish, pull a small crankbait over the top of submerged grass. Occasionally, stop the retrieve, letting the bait float toward the surface. Bass can't resist the slow rise.

FISH ALONG the deep side of a weak break, pitching to the holes near the edges for the best success.

rod to help control the depth, and I keep pulling it through. I take up slack with the reel, but use the rod tip to move the bait and 'finesse' it through the weeds."

HOLE PITCHING

A jig is a great way to catch big bass along the outer weedlines from spring through fall, but it can be painstakingly slow. And if you're trying to pattern bass on a bright, postcold-front day, the technique can be like hunting needles in haystacks.

Not for Minnesota pro Jim Moynagh, who goes hole pitching when the bass have seemingly disappeared.

Moynagh targets the thick beds of milfoil that drape the surface along dropoffs, pitching a jig tipped with a plastic trailer into smaller holes of the weeds. The technique also pays off with pegged plastic worms.

"This works best in clear water where the bass can see the bait after it penetrates the matted surface," he describes. The advantage of hole pitching is that it enables you to present a lure vertically in places where other baits can't be worked effectively.

Moynagh eases along the deep side of a weed break, pitching to the holes near the edges. He works points, cuts and hard bottom areas more thoroughly, but fishes the entire edge until he develops a pattern.

"For whatever reason, the bass will group in a small area, so if you catch one, work that area carefully," he advises.

Moynagh uses 1/2- to 1-ounce jigs that descend quickly and enable him to cover more water. "I jiggle the bait a few times, hesitate, wind it in fast, then pitch to another hole," he describes. "Since most strikes occur as soon as the bait hits bottom, I don't spend a lot of time in each hole."

Moynagh will reduce the jig size if he suspects that bass are suspended off the bottom.

"If you get a strike before the lure hits bottom, that's an indication that a lighter, slower falling jig may be better because it stays above the fish longer," he explains. "Also, if the bottom is supersoft and has a lot of scummy weeds growing on it, I'll use the lighter jig to keep it from sinking into bottom weeds where the bass can't see it."

SPINNERBAIT PUMPING

Because of its weedless nature, the spinnerbait may be the most popular lure for fishing over grassbeds. But sometimes the bigger bass are holding in isolated weed clumps in deeper water — places other anglers often overlook.

That technique works well in South Carolina where BASS pro Scott Martin works a heavy spinnerbait parallel to the deep grass edges of Lake Murray.

"It's a great prespawn technique, especially when the water is cold," Martin explains. "You can use crankbaits in warmer water, but when the water temperature is below 50 degrees, the spinnerbait is deadly."

Martin locates the deep edge where the grass stops growing, and makes long casts with a 1-ounce lure that he winds slowly along the bottom.

"You want to tick grass so that you know you're near the area the bass are likely to be," he describes. "When the bait catches grass, give it a jerk to make it jump. That draws violent strikes."

Martin prefers willowleaf blades in clear water but will opt for big Colorado or Indiana blades in stained or muddy water.

SLOW FALLING WORMS

Topwaters are great choices for shallow weedbeds, but when the weeds are matted near the surface, treble-hook plugs foul easily.

That's when the floating worm can be deadly. You can work it near the surface or allow it to sink into pockets. For whatever reason, it's a bait that bass can't seem to ignore.

"This is a great technique for the postspawn period when bass have pulled away from the banks and are holding in heavy cover," says Stricker. "You can use soft jerkbaits, but I prefer the worm because it's more subtle, and I don't seem to miss or lose as many fish with it."

Stricker fishes bright colored floaters on medium-heavy spinning gear and 12-pound line. He attaches a barrel swivel (to reduce line twist and add casting weight) to the main line and ties a 12-inch leader ahead of the weightless worm.

Stricker casts beyond holes in the weeds and twitches the bait into the opening. If that doesn't elicit a response, he lets it sink beneath the surface, where most strikes occur.

PRECISE presentations are required when bass aren't in the mood to chase baits. Jigs and worms fished vertically will do the trick.

As a tournament fisherman and guide on California's Clear Lake, Jim Munk has learned how to reduce grassbeds to the bare necessities. Instead of making repeated casts to large beds, Munk has developed a highly efficient strategy of targeting fish under the smallest grass patches.

"The ideal weed patch is actually only three or four times bigger than the fish itself. Under the right conditions, these small clumps will isolate quality fish and make every cast count," notes Munk.

"Look for them in cuts or pockets that may be no bigger than a bass boat, just inside a main point. In most cases, I prefer at least 2 feet of water under the clumps."

In most cases, this is an early summer to early fall affair. It works best when water temperatures rise above 80 degrees and the high sun of midday locks fish under these ambush patches. Because the best areas with the best patches are well protected from the wind, about the only condition that causes these patch bass to roam away from the cover — and disrupt the pattern — is cloudy weather.

Whether ringed with tules or brush, the backs of these cuts should feature a small gap of open water between the bank and the grass patches. It is to this target zone that Munk makes relatively short pitches with either a standard Snagproof frog or the new, larger Frogzilla model, walking them like a Zara Spook from the back of the cut out to the grass patch.

"If the fish are very aggressive early in the season, they'll come out after the bait before it ever reaches the grass clump," he says. "As the weather warms — particularly at midday — the strikes often come from right over the patches.

"When you pull the frog up to the patch, you need to let it sit for four or five seconds. Pull it up on the clump and wait again. Pause it the same way when you pull it off the grass. In my experience, most of my quality strikes come during this deadsticking portion of the retrieve."

THE ART OF READING HYDRILLA

This exotic weed is a tremendous bass magnet

MOST BASS ENTHUSIASTS love hydrilla — as long as it is visible and has well-defined edges. That is one reason why there are so many hydrilla experts in the spring of the year.

But there is a real art to "reading" hydrilla throughout the year, particularly when it is deep and submerged. That is a whole new game.

Hydrilla, a fast growing, stalked vegetation with tiny leaves, is an exotic visitor to our waters. Bass anglers are well aware of its ability to supercharge the waters it invades. It is no accident that most of the best bass factories in America have loads of hydrilla: Seminole, Okeechobee, the Santee Cooper lakes, Toledo Bend, Rayburn, Lake Fork, and the Potomac River — among many others.

And deep hydrilla is a wondrous environment where both bass and bass fishermen can spend the entire year.

"I've always believed that the deeper grass is just a magnet to bass," claims Georgia pro Tom Mann Jr. "It is a magnet to bait and a magnet to bass. It is the perfect situation for bass.

"Yet, the average fisherman isn't very good at fishing deep grass. He's intimidated by it. The key is to read it like any other structure. Grass is just another type of structure. Structure is structure, whether it is a weedbed, boat house, brush-pile, stumps, rocks or whatever. Bass are going to relate to it the same way."

"Fishing deep hydrilla takes a lot of patience," adds Ken Ellis, a long time guide on Santee Cooper. "You are subject to fish for several hours without a bite and then catch five or six fish that weigh a total of 30 to 40 pounds, in 20 minutes.

"The whole basis to patterning fish in deep hydrilla is knowing a lot about what is under the hydrilla. The same places, the same depressions and little subtle things on the bottom that were good before the hydrilla came, will still be productive."

Texas pro David Wharton, a former guide on hydrilla covered Sam Rayburn Reservoir and one of the country's top grass fishing experts, emphasizes that the first step to fishing vegetation is to understand that the bass will not be scattered throughout this prime habitat. Bass still relate to bottom changes or irregular features — even if the lake bottom is covered with a carpet of hydrilla 20 feet tall.

That is the starting point to deciphering a sea of hydrilla. From here, the experts provide us with some great clues — a road map of sorts — for solving the hydrilla mystery.

• *Think thick* — World champion angler Jay Yelas advises that with hydrilla "there are always patterns within patterns." And one of the most obvious involves the thickest portions of the vegetation, either visible or discernible on a depthfinder.

"Usually the thickest, most prolific hydrilla areas are the patches where the fish will be," says Yelas, who has a degree in fisheries biology. "For some reason, that denser cover just holds fish."

When Rayburn is drawn down in the fall of the year, Wharton records the locations of the thickest portions and follows that map to some of the best fishing available later in the year, when the reservoir returns to normal pool.

• *Freaky edges* — One of the most obvious tactics with visible hydrilla lines is targeting any irregular or unusual feature along the weed edge. The same tried-and-true tactic applies to submerged hydrilla. Experienced electronics users, like Tom Mann, carefully study the report of their trolling motor-mounted transducer for signs of any point, ragged cut or pocket on an otherwise well-defined edge in the weeds.

Another edge hot spot can be where the depth changes slightly.

"You will fish miles and miles of hydrilla flats and, for some reason, some places on the edge will be deeper," Yelas adds. "It may only be deeper for a few yards, but that is where the fish always are."

• *Inside grasslines* — On most large reservoirs whose depths fluctuate regularly, two distinct hydrilla edges will form. In addition to the deep outside edge, a shallow grassline will grow closer to the shoreline. This inside

WHEN BASS ARE roaming the edges of hydrilla beds, a tandem spinnerbait is an excellent tool for locating schools.

grass edge is the key to springtime bass fishing, according to the experts.

This shallow edge makes an ideal stopping point for both pre- and postspawn bass. If it is close enough to the bank, fish will often spawn along its open water side. And it is usually sparse

enough to accommodate a crankbait, spinnerbait or Carolina rigged plastic bait.

• *Get the point* — There are two kinds of points that hydrilla bass are drawn to — lake bottom contour points and grassbeds that form distinctive points.

A point formed by the bottom contour offers several key spots — identifiable on your depthfinder — that concentrate bass. Look for high spots and dips, drains and depressions, and other forms of cover, like wood and rocks.

The type of point that really makes David Wharton's eyes light up is one formed by a sharp extension of the grassbed itself. Wharton expects to find resident bass relating to the very end of that type of grass point.

• *Current and hydrilla* — When dealing with submerged hydrilla, most fishermen give little consideration to the influence of current on bass in the deep vegetation.

"Any place that current and hydrilla come together are key places," Ken Ellis says. "This is particularly true in the hotter months of the year."

"Current is a big key with grass fishing, and any time you have current, the bass in the hydrilla are going to relate to that current," Mann agrees. "In other words, if you are fishing a main river channel and fishing the downcurrent side of the grass, the fish are going to be facing into the current because the baitfish always wash down with the current.

"With hydrilla and current, you need to concentrate on the eddy-type places around the back sides of points of grass or any place where the current is broken. The fish will be slightly out of the current, but facing into it to ambush bait."

• *Channeling for bass* — Creek channels are usually the highways utilized by bass as they make

Hydrilla and similar water weeds provide various hideouts for bass, including (from top) tunnels formed at drains, the bottom "edge" of weeds, dropoffs formed where plants lead over a channel edge, where wood and weeds meet, and beneath thick surface mats.

Understanding The Growth Stages of Hydrilla

Veteran Florida pro and past Bass-master Classic qualifier Bernie Schultz believes strongly that a little biology lesson is in order when attempting to understand the intricacies of a plant that is capable of growing an inch per day.

"Hydrilla goes through definite growth stages, which can be exploited in different ways," explains Schultz, who mastered hydrilla fishing on weed choked Lake Lochloosa near Gainesville. "The growth stage will dictate how the fish relate to it."

Here is how Schultz describes the various stages of hydrilla growth:

■ **Adolescent Stage** — The first stage after the plant's winter die-off is the Adolescent Stage, which usually lasts for a couple of months. At this stage the plant is between 5 and 30 inches in height and little more than wispy, free-standing fingers of grass.

■ **Crown Stage** — In this stage, which usually occurs through the three months of spring, the hydrilla fingers have grown to the surface and are just beginning to curl over the top of the water. At this stage, the plant is almost fully developed and its stalks become too thick for many lures and techniques.

■ **Matted Stage** — In summer, hydrilla reaches its full maturity and blankets the surface. While it still remains rooted in the bottom, there usually will be huge openings in the grass.

■ **Cavern Stage** — In the late summer and early fall, hydrilla begins the downward side of its cycle. During this time, the plant actually smothers itself. This stage of the plant's growth is characterized by huge mats of hydrilla, which block sunlight from its stalks, killing that portion of the plant. While hydrilla can remain alive for several months despite being detached from the lake bottom, it creates huge open water domes or caverns that provide shade from the intense summer heat, and harbor large numbers of bass.

■ **Dying Stage** — The final stage of hydrilla's growth, this is when the vegetation has begun to disappear. It leaves behind large, open pockets usually inhabited by schooling bass that are foraging for food around the plants.

their seasonal migrations, as well as their temporary homes between movements. It is no different when the surrounding terrain is submerged vegetation.

Yelas and others know that a creek channel that winds through a hydrilla flat is a dependable place to fish throughout the year. And it is the stage for a variety of "a-pattern-within-a-pattern" spots, including bends, high and low areas and rocky or wood laden patches.

A SPINNERBAIT allowed to flutter through openings in hydrilla is a lethal weapon for summoning bass in the grass.

• *Tunnels for bass* — The so-called hydrilla tunnels are what separate the grass specialists from the rest of us. It requires considerable skill at interpreting depthfinding electronics.

"Tunnels are really hard to find, but they are well worth the effort," Wharton says. "These are the kinds of subtle places that you can have all to yourself.

"The fish relate to the bottom as much as they do to the grass. And tunnels are formed by little bottom changes, like a little ditch that goes through a hydrilla flat. The hydrilla doesn't grow in the ditch. What happens is that the hydrilla grows to a certain point and then folds over. When hydrilla on both sides of these small ditches folds over, it creates a tunnel of grass with a void area beneath it. Bass love these tunnels."

THE LAST REMAINING green weeds can provide excellent bass fishing as winter approaches.

WHEN THE VEGETATION DIES
As grass turns brown, bass change patterns

ANGLERS WHO FREQUENT weedy lakes know that bass thrive around aquatic vegetation.

In weedbeds the fish find the forage, cover and oxygen they need for survival. Indeed, many of the best bass fisheries in the nation are chockfull of weeds.

The rapid spread of imported aquatic plants, including Eurasian milfoil, hydrilla and water hyacinths, has turned many over-the-hill lakes and reservoirs into lunker factories. Likewise, waters rich in native plants, such as water lilies, coontail and eelgrass, provide excellent bass action, even in northern states with a short growing season.

Little wonder, then, that fishermen who have spent time mastering weedy patterns may be a bit perplexed when aquatic vegetation starts to die. Weedy lakes can get very tough in late fall or winter as the plants go through their natural die-back cycle. And more than one summer angler, including many top BASS pros, has been on grass bass big time, only to see his pattern trashed by a weed sprayer.

Where do bass go when their weedy lairs disappear? How can anglers locate the last remaining beds of submerged vegetation? Read on for the answers to these sometimes perplexing questions.

(Opposite Page) THE METABOLISM of a bass will diminish as weeds die off. As a result, methodical presentations, like pitching jigs, are effective techniques for catching fish.

USE A CRANKBAIT in the early stages of a die-off to hunt for weed growth areas.

PROFESSOR'S NOTEBOOK

Doug Hannon, Florida's "Bass Professor," is convinced that weedy lakes offer today's best bass fishing. He's made the study of aquatic plants an integral part of his fishing career, and has documented their importance in his books, videos and ESPN television segments.

"In the natural order of things, the growth and death of all vegetation, whether terrestrial or aquatic, is cyclical," says Hannon. "Plant die-off doesn't occur only in cold weather. Even in midsummer, some plants in the lake are blooming while others are dying."

In all but the most tropical climates, aquatic plants undergo a natural "winter

THE CLEARER the water, the deeper you should expect to find fish during the winter weed die-off.

kill," or down cycle, as cold weather sets in, forcing Hannon to change his approach.

"Cooling water, coupled with a lower sun angle resulting in shorter days and diminished solar penetration, slows the metabolism of the plants," he says. "Depending upon the severity of the winter, they will either grow very slowly, remaining green but dormant like lettuce in a refrigerator, or they will die."

Savvy anglers know that healthy aquatic plants produce oxygen, which is necessary for the survival of fish life. Winter plant die-off could thus be a potential disaster in a weedy lake, but nature has a way of preparing fish for the cyclical demise of the plants, Hannon says.

"In winter, the lake's ecosystem is set up to accommodate the die-off of aquatic plants," he adds. "As the metabolism of the weeds lowers, so does the metabolism of the fish and forage species in the lake. As a result, their demand for oxygen drops with every decline in water temperature. In 45 degree water, a bass needs only 20 percent of the oxygen it needed in 75 degree water."

It's when an "unscheduled" die-off occurs, however, that the lake may be thrown into turmoil.

"Spraying or weed harvesting is totally different than normal seasonal weed die-off," Hannon says. "In human terms, weed spraying is like having a bulldozer knock down your house while you're sitting in your living room watching TV. Fish using the weeds aren't prepared to deal with the sudden loss of habitat."

Spraying weeds in warm water leads to excessive decomposition, which consumes vast amounts of oxygen, Hannon notes. "All those dying plants turn to nutrient in the water, which often takes the form of a massive algae bloom. Then, when it's cloudy for a few days, the algae dies and the lake suffers oxygen depletion."

In the seasonal winter die-off, aquatic plants don't disappear all at once. "Shallow emergent plants, including lily pads, rice, maidencane and bulrushes, are the first to go, and the die-off works its way gradually outward to deeper water, following the natural contours of the lake. Deeper grasses, like hydrilla, milfoil, eelgrass and coontail, will be slower to die off, and may stay green all winter in some areas."

DEARMAN'S TIPS

The last green weeds in the lake should always be targeted by serious bass hunters in late fall and winter, believes veteran Texas BASS pro Randy Dearman.

"As the water cools and the grass gets harder to find, its attraction increases," he elaborates. "It seems the less there is of it, the more important each little bit becomes. If you can find a small, isolated patch of green grass in winter, you can make a real bass haul. It can pull in every bass in the vicinity."

Dearman uses a deep diving crankbait to hunt for green growth. He targets areas with the highest potential for living weeds and runs a crankbait through them, dredging bottom for evidence of living grass.

"I want to stay as far away from the dead stuff as I can — dying grass depletes oxygen, while living grass restores it. Plus, living vegetation provides

Where To Find Bass When Grass Is Dead

■ **Hyacinth mats** — Most anglers routinely ignore these floating exotic plants, but Randy Dearman finds them especially important in late fall. "Like lily pads, they provide tremendous shade, but because they aren't rooted to the bottom, they aren't locked into the shallows and can therefore survive the first wave of plant die-off as the water cools. They'll drift into deep coves and river bends and provide super cover for bass." Hyacinths are extremely hardy, Dearman says. "It takes a hard freeze or spraying to kill them. Fish suspend under hyacinth mats, feeding on forage fish that congregate around the plants' dangling roots. Use a push pole to maneuver your boat into the deepest recesses of the floating mat and drop slow falling worms and jigs through the plants."

■ **Deep humps** — "Say you have a hump that tops out at 18 feet," suggests Dearman. "As the lake lowers in late fall, the top gets closer to the surface, receiving increased solar penetration, and may support a good patch of weeds. By the end of drawdown, weeds in the shallows will be dead, but those on top of the hump may be thriving."

■ **Gradual slopes** — "Avoid sharp ledges and dropoffs when hunting green growth late in the season," Doug Hannon recommends. "My favorite structure in late fall is a big, main lake flat. I'll probe remaining weedbeds down to about 15 feet until the water temperature drops into the low 50s, and then shift to sharper dropoffs and a normal winter pattern."

■ **Northern shore** — "Late in the year, you'll find the richest green growth on the northern side of the lake," says Hannon. "Cold, northerly winds that chill the water blow over this area and hit with the most severity on the opposite shore. Also, the sun's lower angle will throw more light on the northern shore than elsewhere."

■ **Ditches and channels** — "As grass dies back after spraying or during late fall, bass will use the small channels and ditches running through the beds as escape routes to deeper winter structure," Dearman advises. "Target these with a deep running crankbait."

■ **Isolated high spots** — "These are dream places if you can find them, for they're often full of thick grass, even when grass elsewhere has died back," Dearman says. "Plus, their proximity to deep, open water leaves them unmolested by weed sprayers. I like to find a small, shallow spot with 20-foot water all around it."

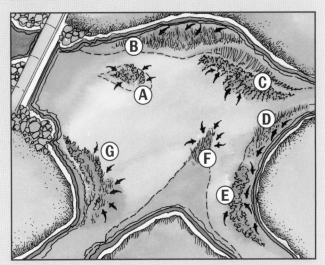

Among hot spots for bass in weedy lakes: **(A)** weed patch on submerged hump; **(B)** inner portions of a large, shallow weedbed where grass is still green; **(C)** secondary ledge with weeds; **(D)** inundated plant stems — good in spring when the lake rises; **(E)** hyacinth mat over deeper water; **(F)** isolated deep weedbed on point; and **(G)** outside edges of weeds that have been sprayed.

more cover for fish and bait because it stands up off the bottom, while dead vegetation lays over and provides little cover."

The clearer the water, the deeper Dearman expects to find living grass late in the season. "More light penetration equals a greater chance for weed survival when the days are short," he says. "I like to hunt up the deepest, greenest grass I can find."

Dead grass, especially dead hydrilla, often breaks loose and floats to the surface.

"If I'm running the lake and start spotting floating dead grass, I'll often stop and check underneath it with my crankbait," he explains. "Often I'll dredge up some green growth along with the dead stuff. Targeting that last little green patch can put you in the money."

Plant-eating water birds are another clue that green grass grows on the bottom, Dearman has found. "If I see a patch of coots on the water and notice some of them diving under, I'll fish this area. They're feeding on the tender green growth on the bottom," he says.

SHIFTING PATTERNS

Any die-off of aquatic vegetation, whether caused by winter-kill, drawdown, drought or spraying, causes bass to relocate. Stay a cast ahead of your competition by taking the advice of our experts. Hunt up any remaining living grass, for it's a surefire bass magnet. Probe the deeper recesses of larger grassbeds. Use a patient approach to match the diminished activity level of the bass. And rest assured that the lake's vegetation will be back to full bloom before too long.

WOOD COVER

Visible to the eye or not,
wood cover holds bass
year-round . . .

THESE STUMPS,
which were exposed
during the drawdown
of a Florida lake,
prove why they are
so attractive to bass.

A SEASONAL GUIDE TO FISHING STUMPS

Find the right stumps in the right locations,
and you'll have a year-round fish factory

IT IS DIFFICULT TO PIN DOWN a veteran tournament pro or guide to one absolute favorite anything when it comes to the sport of bass fishing.

Favorite lure? You will get a wide variety of answers. Favorite technique? You'll hear plenty about versatility and everything from finessing tubes to pitching jigs in heavy cover. Favorite rod? This will elicit an avalanche of varied responses.

But ask a knowledgeable, experienced angler to name the universally preferred cover of both bass and bass fishermen, and one answer will likely dominate — stumps.

"We all know that bass seek cover," Arkansas pro Larry Nixon says, "whatever cover a lake has. But if there are stumps present, the bass are going

to be on them year-round. Stumps are a universal cover for bass."

"In my book, stumps rank as the No. 1 shallow water habitat for bass," agrees Alabama guide Troy Jens, who operates on lakes Guntersville, Neely Henry, Wilson and Wheeler. "But they don't have to be in shallow water to be productive.

"Stumps provide solid cover that's always going to be there. It's one of the few types of permanent cover that bass have. Stumps aren't like laydowns and brush that can be washed away with the current. Stumps are something that the fish can always depend on being there. Plus, stumps provide more shade than most types of cover."

Typically, stumps are 1 to 3 feet in diameter and feature a squat section of trunk that gives way to a network of roots attached to the lake bottom.

The trunk provides plenty of cover for bass, and the root system usually offers ample room for shelter as the bottom erodes away beneath it. The top of the stump is often slick with algae, which attracts baitfish.

"Certain areas of a lake that have stumps are always good," advises Nixon, one of pro bass fishing's most successful and decorated millionaires. "They're good year after year after year. There may be periods when certain stumps are not as good as others, but if you lay off them for two or three weeks and nobody fishes them, you can go right back in there and find the fish stacked up again."

Not all stumps were created equal.

"Some types of stumps are just better than others," says Bill Dance, popular television fishing host and BASS legend. "You can catch bass

BILL DANCE is an advocate of cranking lipped baits into stumps to draw reaction strikes.

around any stump, but to save time and quickly cover more water, you should concentrate on fishing stumps that are positioned on or near dropoffs. These stumps will usually produce better year-round than shallow water stumps.

"Also, keep in mind that the fewer the stumps, the more concentrated the bass should be. If you begin catching fish in a small section of stumps and snag your lure, don't go after it. Let it stay there for a while and use another rig until you've worked the area thoroughly. Then go retrieve your lure. Stump bass spook easily."

LOOK FOR STUMPS near dropoffs, either along creek channels (left) or on points near the main channel.

Dance has found that on lakes with fluctuating water levels, stumps on the southern side of the

body of water will usually be more productive. That's because stumps on the downwind side (from prevailing north winds) are washed more severely when lakes are drawn down in winter. This causes the lake bottom to be eroded, exposing root systems that provide an "umbrella" for bass.

He also advises that stump laden points and flats can often be located simply by studying the shoreline. Stumps on the bank usually indicate stumps under the water. Submerged cover also can be found by fan casting around such areas until your lure pinpoints the objects. And shallow stumps can often be spotted through quality polarized sunglasses, especially if you can keep the sun behind you during your search.

Obviously, locating and fishing visible stumps is considerably easier.

"With visible stumps, experience has taught me that the shady side of the stump is usually better than the brighter side," Dance adds. "My first cast is always to the shady side. And it's very important to cast a few feet beyond the stump. The bass might not be right on the stump, but it should be close by. By casting past the stump, you can cover the back, one side and the front with a single cast. If the lure plops down directly on top of the bass, though, it is likely to be scared away."

The number of casts he makes to a stump depends on several factors, including its depth.

"If it's a key stump on or near a dropoff or a point stump, I'll make several casts with different lures," he explains. "I'll crankbait both sides of the stump a couple of times, for example, while varying my retrieve. Then I'll flip a plastic worm to both sides before moving on."

If pinned down to a single lure for working stumps, both Larry Nixon and Troy Jens would select a rubber-skirted jig with a plastic crawfish trailer. In Nixon's mind there is no better choice for precisely covering a stumpfield than a 1/2-ounce rattling jig with a craw worm trailer. Make a quiet pitch to the base of a stump, pop it off the bottom a time or two, and "if there is a fish there, he will bite it," he declares.

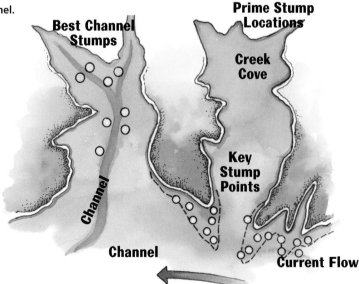

Prime Stump Locations

Best Channel Stumps

Creek Cove

Channel

Key Stump Points

Channel

Current Flow

When fishing for shallow, wary stump bass, Nixon often resorts to Texas rigging a craw worm with a 1/8-ounce weight and 10-pound-test monofilament. He has enjoyed good tournament success in lakes like Guntersville by making long casts to stumps in 1 to 3 feet of water and finessing resident bass into cooperating.

During the summer, Jens uses a variety of lures to hunt down bass on shallow stumps and grass flats, including a 10-inch plastic worm, 3/8-ounce jig, spinnerbait and buzzbait.

"Regardless of the lure I'm using, I always try to position my boat in the channel or out off the ledge," Dance notes. "I cast toward the stump and work the lure from shallow to deep. I honestly believe you will greatly increase your strikes by doing it this way.

"There will be times, though, when the bass will be suspended off the ledge and away from the stumps. In that situation, you can't catch them by fishing shallow to deep. You have to move up on the ledge and fish deep to shallow. And there is an advantage to positioning your boat shallow and casting out into deeper water that occurs once you have hooked a bass. There is a tendency for other bass to follow a hooked fish. By pulling the bass from deep to shallow, the trailing bass move a certain distance, but then quickly return to their original location. When you hook a bass and bring it out over the deeper water, the following fish become disoriented, and it takes them much longer to regroup to their original spot.

"I've seen this happen many, many times. I'm convinced that you will catch more fish from a deep water area by fishing from shallow to deep."

Jens wholeheartedly agrees with that particular Dance lesson. And he also shares the same year-round affinity for stump fishing.

"I can't think of a time of year when I would not fish stumps," he states. "It's a place that will always hold fish. You can count on bass being around stumps, whether they are in shallow water, deep water or in between."

Stumps By The Season

BASS superstar Larry Nixon notes that bass often change preferences for the types of stumps they use at various times of the year. The savvy angler must know when and how to adjust to those preferences.

■ **Prespawn** — Both individual stumps and stumpfields located in deeper water adjacent to a spawning flat concentrate female bass in the early spring in fairly predictable places. As the water warms up, the bass leave their winter locations and migrate to any middepth cover that will provide shelter and slightly warmer water. Stumps fit that criterion perfectly and provide ideal staging areas.

■ **Spawning season** — Stumps positioned on any shallow flat that is somewhat protected from the wind provide excellent spawning cover. Bass often spawn at the base of the roots, and sometimes on top of the stump.

■ **Postspawn** — After spawning is completed, most bass will return to the same middepth stumps that served as a prespawn area.

■ **Summer** — Nixon targets stumps positioned on or near the main river ledges or along creek channels. In this season, the thermocline (the thermal layer in the water column where oxygen levels are highest) comes into play.

"The key is finding a breakline in a certain depth of water where the thermocline is right and baitfish are present," he states. "In most situations in the summertime, 10 to 18 feet is a good depth range on any lake. If you happen to find stumps on a break — like maybe at a creek junction or a little indentation in the deep water where it runs up onto a shallow flat — you're going to find bass."

■ **Fall** — In early fall, Nixon looks for stump bass to be relating to any type of deep channel. But as the water cools, he follows the fish into shallow stumpfields located in the backs of pockets, coves and creeks. "In that situation, anywhere you find even the slightest depression meandering through those stumps, you might just find a gold mine," he says.

■ **Winter** — This is the time of year when Nixon focuses on isolated stumps rather than clusters of cover. Experience has shown him that, during the coldest months, bass relate more to bait than to cover. So he searches for deep, individual stumps along ledges and channels.

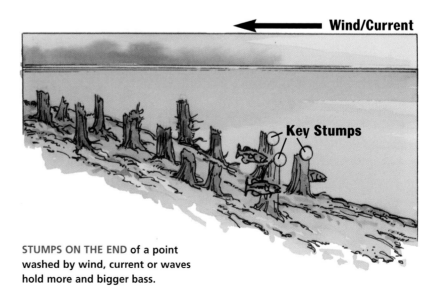

Wind/Current

Key Stumps

STUMPS ON THE END of a point washed by wind, current or waves hold more and bigger bass.

LEARNING HOW to "read" trees is a key to unlocking the secrets of fishing standing timber.

THE WOOD WORKERS
Here's how two top pro anglers find bass in a forest of standing timber

IN MOST CASES, seeing the forest instead of the trees is a good thing. But in the life of a bass fisherman, there are times when the forest actually blocks the view.

With standing timber, every submerged tree adds to what can already be an overwhelming visual puzzle. Even to veteran anglers, a lake filled with timber can produce a very real case of sensory overload. After all, where do you start? What are the key areas? Which lure to use? The questions stack up neater (and certainly faster) than Vegas gambling chips.

1. Forget the trees, check the calendar — While there are a number of subtle nuances to fishing timber, the most critical methods to this fishing madness are big picture items. Specifically, ones that involve not seeing the forest, but ignoring it. Instead of being confused by thickets of flooded timber, a fisherman's initial step should be to treat the lake as if it were devoid of trees and simply focus on the prevailing seasonal pattern.

What time of the year is it? What mode are the fish in? These are the questions that BASS points titleholder and world champion Davy Hite asks himself before all others. To him, whenever standing timber is available, there is no question that this formidable structure for bass will be high on his "to-do" list. About the only thing that might deter these plans is the presence of grass, which generally doesn't provoke much soul-searching, notes Hite, since most lakes seem to have one or the other.

By keying on the seasonal pattern, Hite eliminates much of the timber from consideration simply by its location. If it's not in the right area of the lake or not on the right structure in that area, Hite can effectively ignore a large part of the "forest."

Another angler well-schooled in the ways of wood is Texan David Wharton, someone who cautions fishermen that learning what to ignore and what not to ignore is the real secret to understanding timber.

"In a certain way, you do ignore the trees so you can focus on the bottom structure — what you're looking for is anything different on the

(Opposite Page) THE SIZES of trees can lead anglers to creek channels or other key features holding fish.

FISH JIGGING SPOONS directly over bottom irregularities like humps and ridges when they are covered with standing timber.

river birch, counsels Wharton, a species that doesn't grow anywhere except on a creek bank.

The size of the tree can also lead a fisherman to the creek channel or to other features that may hold fish. In addition to larger trees being found along creek channels, they may also indicate an old fencerow where the line of timber once served as a farmer's windbreak. Or, where a depression or hollow offered ideal growing conditions.

At this point, any body of water has been effectively reduced to manageable proportions by first using the seasonal pattern to select the most attractive section and then using the trees themselves to find the creek channel. For both Hite and Wharton, locating a creek channel is a primary key to finding bass in timber. The time of year dictates how the fish will relate to that channel.

bottom. It just happens to have timber on it," notes Wharton. "To a degree, the trees are telling you what lies below."

2. Find the creek channels — With experience, a skilled angler often can gauge bottom contours by the type and size of tree present. In general terms, this means that you can expect species such as oaks on hard bottom areas, cypress and willows along creek channels or depressions, and pines on sandy ridges or high spots. While there are many variations on these themes, learning the basics of where certain trees are normally found (combined with the idiosyncrasies of each lake) provides even more clues to the timber riddle.

For instance, if you find a combination of cypress trees right next to a group of pines, more than likely there will be a hump or ridge (where the pines are growing) that drops off into a creek channel (bordered by cypress). If you happen to be fishing in east Texas, you might also look for a

3. Find the depth range — The next step in this process of shrinking the lake and the amount of timber fished is to identify the most productive depth range. Although some fish may relate to bottom structure underneath the trees, they will also relate to the trees as the cover on the bottom. The goal is to find the specific position along this vertical cover where the fish feel most comfortable and catchable.

Now, the focus shifts back to the type and size of trees found in this depth range. Depending on how precisely the fish can be patterned, the type of tree (oak, cypress, willow, pine, cedar, etc.) can be a great time saver in locating similar areas around the lake. The size of the tree can also be a tip-off to what the fish prefer, particularly during the spawn when bass actually use the timber itself as a spawning bed. (More on this later.)

4. Catch a fish, pay attention — By factoring in variables like water depth, clarity, fish aggressiveness, time of year and position on timber, lure choices become almost second nature. (For most applications, a basic selection of spinnerbaits, cranks, jigs, plastic worms and spoons will do the job.) Then, it's simply a matter of catching a few fish to get a handle on the prevailing bite.

"When you catch a fish, it's so important to try and develop a pattern no matter what you're doing," counsels Hite. "I mean quality fish — 3-, 4-, 5-, 6-pound fish — not just little bank runners. When you get a good fish or two, you really need to look at that tree, the overall water depth, the depth where the fish was caught, all of that."

5. Don't count on anything — The last item in this process of elimination is simply realizing that nothing with timber is an absolute. While the same could be said of all bass fishing disciplines, standing timber brings so many extra variables into play that it is difficult, if not impossible, to rely on any one rule for every situation. Instead, a fisherman needs to be especially observant with timber and not overlook the subtleties of size, type, shape, thickness, etc., that can mean success or failure.

While the above guidelines remain the same year-round, each season poses a special set of problems for timber fishermen. This is how David Wharton and Davy Hite make sense of it all:

PRESPAWN

No matter the season, Wharton believes that channels and timber go together like a wink and a smile. In the prespawn period, he looks for a channel that runs directly through the timber and is 12 to 15 feet in the middle and 5 to 7 feet on the sides. His primary focus would be the larger hardwood trees along the edge of the creek in shallow water.

Prespawn is perhaps the best time to fish timber, notes Hite, especially for big fish. When the water temperature gets anywhere from 50 to the

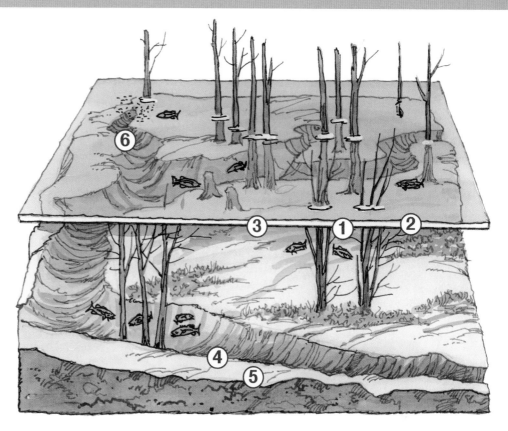

1) PRESPAWN: Channel running directly through timber, 12 to 15 feet in middle, 5 to 7 feet on sides. 2) Spawn: Large trees or stumps on a spawning flat or directly on submerged trees. 3) Postspawn: Follow channel back out, as fish will group on channels or suspend in timber. 4/5) Summer & Winter: Look in creek channels 15 to 25 feet, pay attention to thermoclines. 6) Fall: Find creeks with bait.

mid-60s, he starts looking in the timber, but not necessarily up shallow. Since some bass actually spawn in the wood itself and never go to shore, Hite's choice is often a spinnerbait worked at various depths.

"A big key when the surface is warming quickly is to figure out the fish holding depth in the timber and then work a spinnerbait in that zone. It may require anything from a 1/4-ounce to a 1-ounce lure to achieve the desired result."

Ideally, the best place to locate timber in the prespawn is along a creek channel adjacent to a spawning flat. In these more specific areas, says Hite, a fisherman can really narrow things down and pattern the fish.

WHEN FISHING vertically, Wharton drops his lure directly into treetops. Depending on the condition, strikes can occur anywhere from the top on down. Wharton lets the bait go all the way to the bottom and works it there. If no response, he brings up the lure and tries again, gradually working his way up the tree.

SPAWN

Important keys during this period are the larger trees or stumps in a spawning flat. It's clearly a case of the bigger, the better, notes Wharton, since big trees have big root systems which provide more shallow cover. The bass will move up from the channel and off onto a nearby flat, frequently spawning at the base of these large trees.

If you can't find enough fish up shallow (or places to fish for them), Hite recommends looking for bass that never go shallow to spawn, but simply do their business in the timber itself.

"People don't realize that the whole spawning process can happen right there. The fish basically need horizontal limbs just under the surface down to 4 feet, depending on the water clarity. And the limbs don't have to be all that big, maybe 6 inches or so in diameter. A lot of those limbs will be 18 to 20 inches thick. For the bass, it's like spawning on top of a stump or right on the bottom. You see, they don't need all that much space. Plus, if those fish are born and raised out on that timber, they don't need to migrate all the way to shore."

POSTSPAWN

After the fish leave the beds, Wharton follows them back out to the creek channel, knowing they will generally use the same path out as they used on the way in. Although many bass will group together on these creek channels, some will suspend in the timber. During this period (usually May to June), Wharton employs a shallow running crankbait caromed off stumps or worked along limbs. Occasionally, he turns to topwater baits, such as chuggers and Zara Spooks.

Although postspawn is a productive time for fishing timber, Hite also instructs fishermen to be aware of suspended bass. Typically, it's tougher to catch big fish that have just gone through the spawning process, so he recommends downsizing lures and fishing them more methodically. While finesse tactics can produce fish in timber, admits Hite, his penchant for heavier line keeps him from dropping down too far in line test.

SUMMER

Sticking with a river or creek channel, Wharton will vertically jig deeper treetops in 15 to 25 feet of water. Using a plastic worm or craw worm, he will position himself directly over a thick tree (such as a hardwood or pine) on the edge of a creek channel and drop the bait straight down into it. Depending on the conditions and the mood of the fish, the strikes can come anywhere from the top on down. Since the location and aggressiveness of the fish can change with the day, Wharton advises anglers to change their sinker weight to match the situation.

"I jig the worm just like a spoon and will use anything from a 1/4- to 1/2-ounce sinker. My personal rule for choosing sinker weight is fairly simple — I want to use the lightest sinker possible, one that allows the lure to do what I want it to do."

The presence of a thermocline, a relatively well-defined change in temperature that sets up at a certain depth and congregates both bass and baitfish, is also a concern for Wharton. In extremely hot weather during August and September, these thermal "fences" usually show up at 15 to 25 feet (often deeper in western impoundments) and virtually define the depth range where most fish are located. Fortunately, the presence of vegetation, like hydrilla, in many impoundments has reduced the impact of thermoclines and spread the fish over a broader depth range.

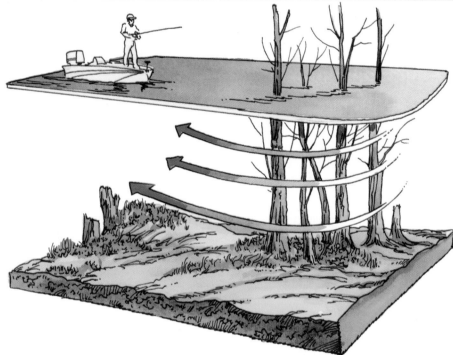

HITE ADJUSTS his search depth by changing his spinnerbait size. Depending on the depth and conditions, it may demand anything from a 1/4-ounce to a 1-ounce lure.

FALL

"The guys who take the time to learn how creek channels bend and wind through a timber flat are the same guys who will catch most of the fish," declares Wharton.

In this search for creek channels, he knows that the larger trees provide a good starting point and offer a tremendous amount of cover at their bases where fallen limbs have collected. In the fall season, Wharton will look for fish moving with bait to the backs of creeks. An early morning topwater attack will later be followed with spinnerbaits.

Since the bass are roaming with the bait, Hite looks for timber with a lot of bait around it. This bait will generally be closer to the surface than in

summer or winter and moving to the backs of the creeks.

WINTER

With fish positioned deeper on river and creek channels, the winter predicament is very similar to that of summer. For Wharton, this means jigging spoons in the treetops — usually in the 20- to 25-foot range.

"I'm just not surprised if I catch them up in the top of a tree, because the fish tend to suspend there quite often. For instance, if I'm fishing in 30 feet of water and there's a little tree that comes up maybe 15 feet off the bottom, I'll drop a jig or worm straight into that tree — and expect it to get bit on the way down.

"If I'm jigging vertically, I'll let the bait go all the way to the bottom and jig it two or three times. If nothing happens, I'll reel it up a little and repeat the procedure all the way up the tree."

Although summer and winter seem very different, they actually demand similar tactics because of the "comfort zones" that hold bass and baitfish. Hite focuses on those trees (such as cypress and willows) that normally identify channels.

LEARN ABOUT LAYDOWNS
Fishing fallen trees is one of the fundamentals of bass fishing

FISHING FALLEN TREES is one of the basics in this sport; these woody skeletons are Everyman's Structure. They are scattered along the banks of lakes and rivers throughout the country. Anybody can find fallen trees by cruising and looking. And virtually every angler can catch bass from them by tossing baits into the limbs and winding them back out. In effect, fishing this cover is fundamental in bassing, like football's off-tackle run or basketball's baseline jumper.

"Fallen timber is one of the best types of cover there is for bass, but fishing it properly is a lot more complicated than most people realize," says former Bassmaster Classic winner Larry Nixon of Bee Branch, Ark. "There are a lot of subtle patterns involved, and fishermen need to be able to figure out these little quirks and then use the baits and techniques that match up with them."

"How good fallen trees are depends on what other cover exists in that lake or river," notes David Wharton of Texas, a full-time pro since 1979. "If they're the primary cover, they can be great. But where there's a lot of aquatic grass, laydowns are less important to bass."

PRESPAWN LOGGIN'

"The prespawn and spawn are my favorite times for fishing fallen trees," Nixon says. "This is when a lot of big bass are up shallow, and they're hungry, so catching them is pretty simple.

"In prespawn, I fish trees that are adjacent to shallow water bays. They may be on the first or second point going into a cove or pocket, somewhere the bass have to pass on the way to their spawning areas. When they come to a fallen tree, they're likely to move into the cover and hold for a few days."

A key this time of year is having deep water (7 to 10 feet) adjacent to the tree.

Wharton likes to fish trees that fall into an old channel or down a deep bank, and they should be toward the mouth of the creek.

Both anglers rely on the same types of lures: a white/chartreuse spinnerbait followed by a blue/black jig-and-pig. And both position their boats several yards from where they think the tree ends and begin fan-casting the limbs with the spinnerbait to pick off active bass.

Wharton slow rolls his spinnerbait through the limbs, letting it fall to 5 or 6 feet deep, and then bumping it through the limbs. Whenever he pulls the spinnerbait over a limb, he quits winding momentarily to let the bait flutter back down.

He fishes the entire tree with the spinnerbait, working his way in on both sides of the trunk, before scraping his bait alongside this main stem. If it's a sunny day, he pays particular attention to shady areas.

After working the tree with the spinnerbait, Nixon slides his boat into pitching/flipping range, and he prospects in every hole and limb fork with the jig-and-pig.

"The fish are usually lying in a place where somebody else hasn't put a bait, so I'll try to determine that spot. Many times, that's where the fish will be."

LOGS IN THE SPAWN

As bass move into shallow water to spawn, fallen trees remain prime fishing structure. Locations and methods change as spring progresses, however.

"When the water hits spawning temperature (mid-60s), concentrate on fallen trees on flats and side pockets, wherever the bass will nest," advises

Nixon. "I like trees in 2 to 5 feet of water, and I concentrate on working the outer limbs. Many times the fish will spawn in the edge of the tree, where sunlight can hit the nest."

The best baits for this type of fishing are a twitch bait (Rapala, Long A Bomber, etc.) and a plastic lizard or jig. The anglers try surface lures first, then follow up with a sinking bait.

AFTER THE SPAWN

Following the spawn, bass begin moving back toward summer holding areas.

Wharton starts in the backs of bays and works his way out. "In the immediate postspawn, bass may still be close to their spawning areas," he says. "A little later, they'll move near the mouths of the creeks or out on the main lake area, where they'll spend the summer."

Just after spawning, expect to find bass tight to the cover, in the heaviest places you can put your bait, Nixon advises. "This type of fishing is usually all worms and lizards and jigs."

However, as the fish rebound from the spawning ordeal, they become more aggressive, and now

the best baits are faster and flashier, matching the fish's warm weather appetite for shad. "By late spring, I'll throw a buzzbait or a topwater, especially early in the morning, then I'll follow up with a crankbait or worm," Wharton says.

Fishing crankbaits through treetops is a special art. To do this, Wharton prefers a buoyant bait with a big bill, which fends limbs away from the hooks. "You can crawl a crankbait through some really heavy cover if you pay attention and work it carefully," he states. "It's more a matter of pulling it with your rod tip than cranking it."

In summer, Wharton continues to fish a spinnerbait, although he prefers a smaller model, such as a 1/4-ounce bait with a small willowleaf blade to match the size of young shad.

Come fall, bass make another migration up the creeks. They especially relate to cover on or near creek channels. "If you can find channel banks that swing in close to the shore, and you have trees lying down these banks in the water, this is usually a key fall pattern," Nixon says. Again, spinnerbaits, crankbaits and worms are the most productive lures in this cooling season.

DURING THE postspawn expect bass to hold tight to thick cover.

BASS IN THE WILLOWS

When willow bushes are flooded in spring, expert anglers know exactly where to go

CERTAIN PAGES OF THE FISHING calendar have an irresistible appeal to bass anglers. Some long for the first warm spell of the year, when big bass move from their winter haunts to shallow staging areas and will respond to a suspending jerkbait. Others anticipate early fall, when bass school on main lake points and will eagerly attack topwater lures.

Many anglers would pick those magic spring days when bass are "up in the willow bushes" as their favorite fishing period. That's the time when shoreline bushes, which remained high and dry during the winter drawdown, are inundated as the reservoir rises following spring downpours. The sudden flooding of the shoreline triggers an annual cycle that can produce some of bass angling's finest moments.

FLOODED WILLOW bushes attract feeding fish, making a spinnerbait or other reaction bait a good choice for catching prespawn bass.

WHY BASS USE FLOODED BUSHES

"Flooded bushes, especially willows and buttonbushes, attract bass for many reasons," says Birmingham, Ala., fisheries biologist and avid bass angler Chris Stephenson. Among them:

• *Cover* — "For their relatively modest size, willow bushes offer a great deal of cover for bass," Stephenson explains. "Willows are ter-restrial plants whose root systems grow just beneath the ground. When they're inundated in a reservoir, the roots are often exposed, presenting bass and their forage with abundant hiding opportunities."

• *Shade* — "Bass, like most predators, conceal themselves in shade, and willow bushes provide excellent shade in shallow water."

• *Forage opportunities* — "Flooded willows provide predatory gamefish with a veritable cafeteria of insects, small baitfish, crawfish and other forage species. Mayflies often hatch out en masse in flooded willows — their larvae live underwater seven years before the adult emerges and takes to the air for 24 hours before dying. Mayfly hatches can provoke monumental feeding frenzies — bluegill and bass will gorge themselves on these winged insects."

• **Spawning area** — "Willows grow in muddy, swampy terrain rather than rocky soil; when the plants are flooded in spring, bass will spawn around them because they can easily fan out a nest on the mud bottom, and because the bush provides a partial barrier to egg predators, such as bluegill. Willows also break up wave action, which allows increased solar penetration for more effective egg incubation."

HOWELL'S WILLOW WISDOM

Alabama pro Randy Howell cut his angling teeth in eastern North Carolina, where sprawling impoundments near its coast are prone to seasonal flooding. His parents owned a marina on Lake Gaston, and he began guiding on the reservoir when only 12 years old. "The spring willow bush pattern is one I look forward to all year long," offers Howell. His biggest largemouth, a 10-pounder, came off a flooded willow on a floating worm. "I skipped the worm under the bush, worked it out about a foot and the bass came out in slow motion and ate it. When I set the hook and it took off, it turned the front end of the boat completely around, it was so big. To actually see a bass that size strike was the thrill of a lifetime," he says.

Although Howell targets flooded bushes under any water condition, his preference is clear water, when he can see his quarry. Using his trolling motor to move quietly within casting range, he keeps his eyes peeled for signs of bass.

Howell scouts for bass cruising the outer

LOOK FOR MATS of floating debris in flooded willows. The denser cover is attractive to the fish.

INSECTS OFTEN HANG on flooded willows in droves. If fish aren't active, swat several bushes with a boat paddle to dislodge bugs and then wait several minutes and cast to the spot.

RANDY HOWELL'S SKIPPING TECHNIQUE

1. Use Polarized sunglasses to spot target.
2. Once target is located, focus on initial impact point ahead of the fish.
3. 6 1/2–foot medium action spinning rod.
4. Use low, sidearm rod swing so worm "whipcracks."
5. 10- to 12-pound mono.
6. Initial impact point.
7. Small willows: bluegill and small bass.
8. Vary intensity of initial contact to control distance/numbers of skips.
9. Floating worm.
10. Big willow: big bass.

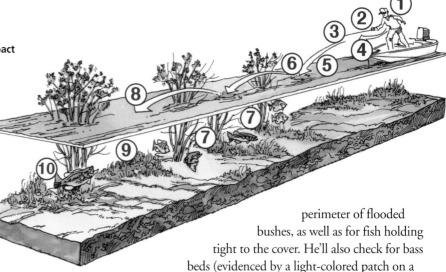

More Tips For Willow Bush Bass

■ On sunny days, make your initial lure presentations to the shady side of flooded bushes, which is where bass are most likely to be holding unless they're actively spawning.

■ Flooded willow bushes are outstanding current breaks in river-run reservoirs. "Bass will typically locate behind the bush, facing into the current, so present your lure upstream and let the current wash it naturally into the strike zone," advises Randy Howell.

■ When heavy with rain, willow bush branches sag into the water, creating even more overhead cover for bass. Use high visibility lures on dark days.

■ Look for debris such as branches or logs trapped in bushy areas during seasonal floods. This cover further enhances the bushes' appeal to bass.

■ If you hang your lure in a bush, don't pull hard — gently shaking the rod tip will usually work the bait free.

■ When using a Texas rigged soft plastic lure in bushes, always peg your sinker or use a screw-in sinker, such as Gambler's Florida Rig. Otherwise the sinker will consistently end up on one side of a limb, with the lure on the other.

■ Don't let the presence of numerous bushes between you and your target intimidate you when skipping a floating worm. "Just do it!" encourages Howell. "Standing there worrying about how you're going to get that worm back where you want it will invariably cause you to flinch and mess up your cast."

■ Insects often hang on flooded bushes in droves. If fish aren't active, swat several bushes with your boat paddle to dislodge insects, wait several minutes, then cast to the spot.

■ Snakes commonly are found in flooded bushes, so use extreme caution when reaching into a bush to free a tangled lure.

perimeter of flooded bushes, as well as for fish holding tight to the cover. He'll also check for bass beds (evidenced by a light-colored patch on a darker bottom), bass fry (a small cloud of tiny fish) or any signs of movement around the bushes.

SKIPPING SAVVY

Not surprisingly, Howell's favorite lure for willow bush bassin' is a floating worm.

"Besides having extra flotation, the worm you use for fishing flooded bushes should be bright enough for both you and the bass to see it," he notes. "Bass are curious and will swim out of the bush and check out a colorful worm, even in very clear water. Usually they'll strike it, but if they hesitate, I'll switch to a more subdued shade, like blue or pumpkinseed."

Howell rigs his floating worms on a 4/0 offset-shank worm hook and stresses the importance of keeping the lure dead-straight on the hook, noting, "A crooked floating worm will result in monumental line twist."

Howell uses a 6 1/2-foot, medium action spinning rod-and-reel outfit for fishing a floating worm. He spools up with 10- or 12-pound-test mono, preferring the latter in superclear water.

Howell's prowess at skipping a floating worm is truly awesome — he can consistently deliver the lure to seemingly inaccessible bushes.

"Most fishermen are content to fish the outer perimeter of the willows, but I've caught most of my big fish deeper within the cover, especially in a

DON'T PULL HARD if your lure gets hung in a bush. Instead, gently shake the rod tip and it will usually free the bait.

tournament situation, where bass are highly pressured," Howell says. "The only possible way to get the lure back where the fish are is to skip it. If you cast overhand to flooded bushes, you'll constantly hang up your line or lure in the branches."

Howell stands and scans the water for signs of bass. If he locates a fish, he makes a low sidearm cast — almost a whipcrack — so the worm hits the water well in front of the target with considerable force, then skips gently into the strike zone.

This is where the right rod is essential: "You need some give to the rod tip to present the worm just right — most fishermen look at all that cover and think they need a real heavy rod, but this won't give you the whip crack effect you need for skipping," he notes. By varying the intensity of the cast and the location of the lure's initial contact point, Howell can skip the worm once, twice or several times before it finally comes to rest.

"Skipping definitely takes practice — there's a certain rhythm to it that's indescribable, but once you 'find the groove,' you can do it every time," he advises.

Once the worm comes to rest, Howell pulls, darts or twitches it away from cover, letting any reaction from the fish determine the speed and activity level of the retrieve.

"Sometimes bass want the worm to twitch actively and move quickly; other times they want it to sink slowly," he adds. "Let the bass tell you how to fish it."

If Howell has a good fish spotted that won't strike his floating worm, he quickly switches to a finesse worm rigged on a lightweight jighead. He casts this right in front of the fish and gently shakes the rod tip so the small lure writhes in place on the bottom. This will often trigger a wary fish to bite.

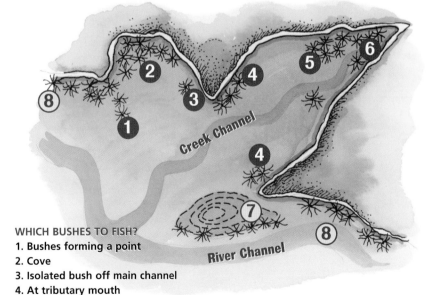

WHICH BUSHES TO FISH?
1. Bushes forming a point
2. Cove
3. Isolated bush off main channel
4. At tributary mouth
5. Along creek channel
6. In back of creek arm
7. Close to hump
8. Close to river channel

⬤ Best in early spring
◯ Best in late spring

HARBORING BASS

Marinas provide varied and relatively untapped hideouts for big bass

P ICK ANY LAUNCH RAMP on just about any day and watch as one bass fisherman after the next motors impatiently to the 5 mph markers and then buries the throttle. Within minutes, the roostertails and throaty growls of outboards disappear, replaced by the daily comings and goings of the marina.

Instead of seeing a marina for what it is — a man-made collection of structure and cover that attracts both predator and prey — these anglers see only the hubbub on the surface.

If the object is to find a quiet cove and spend a bucolic day on the water, so be it. But far too often, bass fishermen run away from marinas for all the wrong reasons. According to professional anglers like Bassmaster Classic champion George Cochran, former BASS tournament big bass record holder Mark Menendez and western superstar Aaron Martens, anglers quite wrongly assume that marinas are (1) too congested, (2) heavily pressured and (3) generally produce small fish.

In the first place, a marina is like any other area of a lake. While it may not be productive all the time, bass in such areas respond to the seasons and can be patterned accordingly.

"When I get in a marina bay, I treat it like a little lake," observes Menendez. "I use the seasonal pattern to pinpoint that portion of the marina most likely to hold fish.

"A marina is a little microcosm, a small environment that offers year-round opportunities. The problem is that marinas are easy to overlook because of the traffic going in and out."

THE COMPONENTS

• *Docks* — The most obvious and significant parts of a marina's landscape are docks. These provide most of the necessary elements to attract bass and baitfish — shade, cover, wood, brush and structure. Depending on the season, one or more of these factors is critical, not only in determining where bass will be positioned, but also which presentations are required to make them strike.

For a western fisherman like Martens, cover is welcome anywhere you can find it. Often, it's the result of brush or Christmas trees planted under docks.

(Opposite Page) MARINAS ARE sometimes unknowingly built over inconspicuous bass cover, like humps, ridges and sharply defined dropoffs. The cover they provide is an added bonus for the bass.

A WORM SKIPPED into the shadiest slip of a marina and allowed to fall parallel down a piling is a proven technique for dock fishing.

"If you find something like this, it can be a gold mine," he says. "I have places that I can go to during extremely tough bites, pull up, and get bit immediately. Once you hit that cover, it's automatic. If you have 30 or 40 of those in a big marina, you will be king."

While casting accuracy and correct presentations are always important, nowhere does their significance take on greater meaning than around boat docks. Regardless of where bass are positioned on docks — and no matter if the fish are relating to the bottom or suspended underneath — putting the bait on target is paramount.

"You can't simply throw a lure around these docks and expect to catch bass," counsels Cochran. "You have to put that bait exactly in the strike zone to be successful."

SUNNY, BRIGHT conditions are optimum for dock fishing because the fish seek the shade offered by this man-made structure.

The accuracy required in dock presentations may take several forms. If bass are suspended under a dock (as they are prone to do in summer), the critical zone is often a narrow sliver that runs along the edge of the dock where the sun meets the shade. At other times, getting the bait even farther under a dock is necessary and may require two rods with baits (crankbaits, for example) tuned to run left and right.

Success can often hinge on the ability of an angler to probe areas of marina structure that don't see a lot of lures. Just ask Dion Hibdon, who won the 1997 Classic at Lake Logan Martin in Alabama. He credits his victory to being able to skip spider grubs and tube baits 20 to 25 feet underneath large docks. Consequently, he was catching fish in places where few others had ever put a bait.

In addition to the actual docks, there are two other peripheral components to the big picture of marina fishing.

• *Riprap* — Whether the riprap is composed of large boulders or chunk rock, this structure often borders the outside edges of marinas and serves as prime staging areas for pre- or postspawn bass. They can also hold fish at other times of the year because of the food chain that exists in these areas.

• *Launch ramps* — Perhaps the most routinely overlooked piece of structure in any marina, launch ramps can offer some of the least exploited fishing opportunities. Although the fish may use them more sporadically, they can provide a subtle breakline that is often in close proximity to docks or other types of structure.

THE SEASONS

With man-made influences, marina patterns can offer some unique subtleties that may not be found elsewhere. Even so, the basic guidelines of seasonal patterns can greatly narrow the playing field and place an angler in the most productive area.

Then, the process of finding the daily pattern is much the same as it would be in other parts of the lake. By catching one or two bass, observing their positions around structure or cover and how they want the bait presented, you can pattern marina bass in similar locations all around the harbor.

However, marina bass, notes Martens, can move around somewhat from day to day (depending on the season and particularly in clear water conditions), so it may require some adjustments in precisely where and how a fisherman presents his lure.

• *Late winter/early spring* — As the seasons transition from late winter to early spring, the first places to look for warmer water are those that help the process along. Specifically, riprap areas at the mouths of marinas, concrete seawalls and similar structure where prespawn bass can benefit from the reflected heat. Ideally, marinas located on the northeastern shoreline (which receive the most direct sunlight in the early season) would be the first choice.

Suspending jerkbaits or lightweight jig-and-pigs that can be fished over broken rock will be most effective on staging fish. This is also one of the key times for crankbaits, since riprap areas (places where crankbaits can impact and deflect off structure) clearly offer some of the best opportunities in a marina.

More Tips
For Dock Fishing

■ Permanent docks supported by large posts usually are found in shallow water and provide more options for fish because of the size of the posts and the amount of shade they produce. Bass hanging around floating docks — typically used along deeper banks — tend to suspend in the top 5 feet of water. Anglers often ignore the walkway bridging the floating dock and shoreline, yet it attracts bass when they are shallow, especially during the spawning season.

■ Pay attention to where you're catching fish around the docks. If you catch a couple of bass from the back corners of a dock, chances are that's where you'll find bass holding on other docks.

■ Accuracy is critical to successful dock fishing. Also, bass will spook easily in clear water and lose their aggressive instincts if a lure makes a lot of noise upon entry.

■ Cloudy skies hamper dock fishing because the fish roam away from the cover. However, a sunny, windless day positions fish under the docks, where they are easier to target. In fact, bluebird skies and cold front days make good dock days.

■ If the docks are getting a lot of pressure from anglers, note how others are fishing them, and do something different. For example, if they're sitting on the deep outside edge and casting to the side of the dock, move to the shallow side and cast toward deep water. If everyone is throwing jigs or worms, try pitching a crankbait or spinnerbait.

• *Spring* — In spring, the emphasis shifts to shallow water zones in the backs of marinas, particularly pea gravel areas on side points and pockets. Another key area for spawning fish is often located directly behind docks in shallow water.

Depending on the cover available, many of the same lures that work elsewhere on a lake (such as Texas rigged lizards) are also highly effective in marinas. If water clarity permits, sight fishing can be exceptional. Whatever the conditions allow, bass that use a marina the rest of the year also take advantage of its stable conditions during the spawn.

• *Summer* — More than anything else, shade dictates the summertime bite as the bass suspend and position themselves along the edges of docks or under large boats. As the season progresses, the fish tend to move farther out toward the ends of docks, especially those positioned over deeper water. In all of these dock fishing situations, the emphasis is squarely on making the right presentation to fish that are willing to ambush prey, but need some coaxing to do so.

Summer is the season when making the right casts (and having the courage to worry more about where to put the lure and less about getting a fish out) spells the difference between someone who dabbles in a marina and someone who truly takes advantage of the situation.

• *Fall* — When baitfish start moving around in fall, the marina fisherman becomes a hunter who needs to focus on areas that collect minnows. In some cases, the presence of baitfish may depend on

a certain bottom composition (such as pea gravel) or it may be dictated by the wind.

In windblown areas, the baitfish will follow plankton into pockets or coves and the bass are sure to follow. The only problem is that such foraging tends to move both prey and predator around, so the "hunting" portion of the program comes into play. As a result, "coverage lures," like spinnerbaits or buzzbaits, are excellent tools for locating bass in the fall and for staying with them.

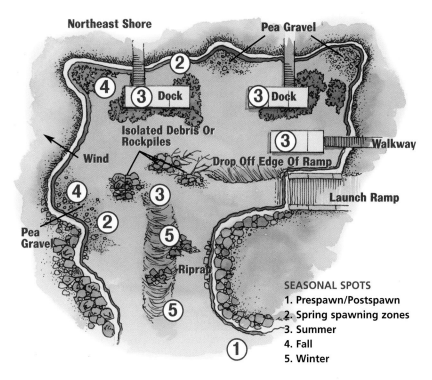

SEASONAL SPOTS
1. Prespawn/Postspawn
2. Spring spawning zones
3. Summer
4. Fall
5. Winter

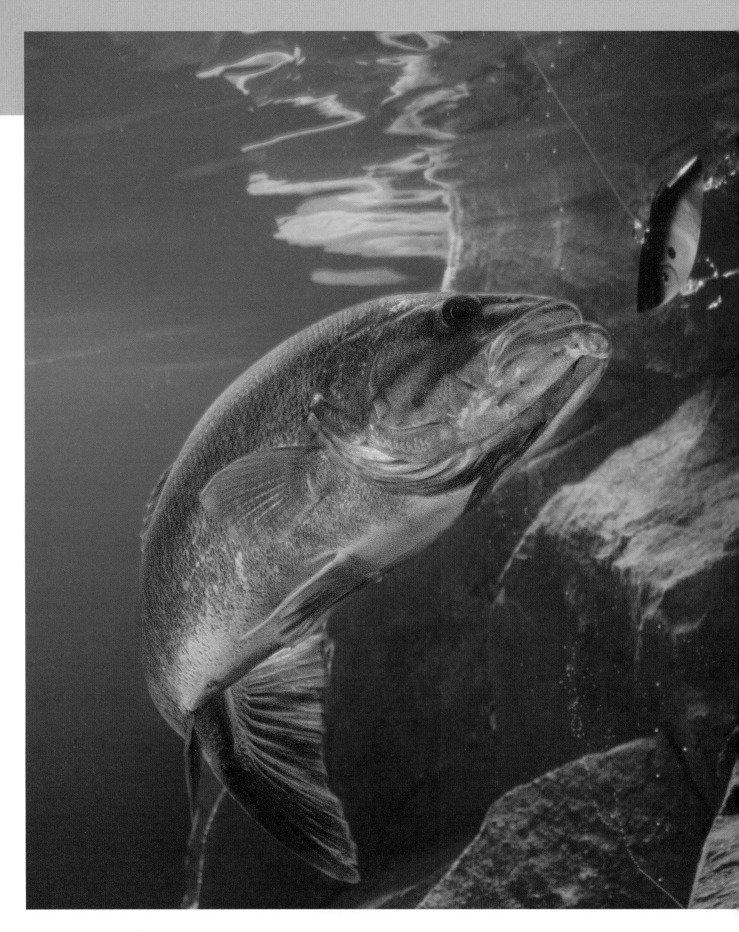

ROCKS

This natural habitat is a proven
producer of quality bass fishing . . .

DURING COOL MONTHS, rocks exposed to sunlight retain heat and warm nearby water, making them especially appealing to the bass.

BASS ON THE ROCKS

Bass may prefer weeds and wood for cover, but you must know how to fish rocks as well

O F THE THREE primary habitats of bass, rocky structure may be the easiest to fish, but it's also the least understood.

With spring being the biggest exception, bass are more predictable when weeds and wood are more readily available. On the other hand, hard bottom patterns are less noticeable, therefore, anglers often overlook them.

If you fish where smallmouth and spotted bass live, knowing how and where to fish rock is essential. To a degree, largemouth tend to be less finicky about bottom content, showing a greater need for cover they can get beneath. However, when rock provides any bass the best option, it will take it.

All bass are attracted to hard bottoms for spawning and feeding. In addition to the obvious — sand, rock and gravel — man-made habitat, such as riprap, seawalls, launch ramps and roadbeds, can be equally attractive.

"Bass also use hard bottoms for staging and migrating during the change of seasons," explains Missouri pro Randy Blaukat. "But rock is no different than other cover in that it must be positioned on the structure properly to be productive. Choose the structure, then look for the cover. A lot of rocks do not make a honey hole. But rocks positioned properly on good structure often do."

What is the appeal? During the cool water seasons, rocks — especially those exposed both above and below the water — retain heat and warm nearby water. That's important to bass and forage during the prespawn period and fall.

Protection can be another factor. Bass will tuck behind big boulders, using them as points of ambush or simply to seek shade on a bright day. On rivers, rocks provide the additional benefit of shelter from the current.

Above all, though, food is what draws bass to rocks. Unlike wood or weeds that rot and deplete oxygen in the water, rock is a continuous food source for minnows and crawfish. Organic material stores in the cracks, which may be one reason why rocky areas can be so productive during late fall and winter.

"Everyone associates crawfish with rocks, but baitfish use them just as often," says Indiana smallmouth expert Greg Mangus. "Look around a launch ramp or seawall or

(Opposite Page)
IF FISH ARE suspended or lethargic, a blade bait jigged vertically along a bluff or steep rock wall can make them bite, especially smallmouth.

Pinpointing Bass On Riprap

Riprap is one of the most identifiable and common rock features on any lake, and it's a structure that will hold bass through all the seasons.

Riprap is a man-made structure, consisting of large chunks of rock or limestone placed along a shoreline to protect it from erosion. You'll find riprap around bridge banks, along the faces of dams, at entrances to marinas and harbors or protecting private shorelines.

Not all riprap banks are equal in bass production. Generally, banks that taper into deep water can pay off year-round because they give bass a variety of depth options.

However, shallow or gradually sloping riprap bottoms can be excellent during early spring and late fall. The large rocks absorb heat from the sun and retain it well. Forage and prespawn bass seeking the warmth will move to those shallow riprap areas and feed there throughout the day.

During summer, bass can be found shallow on steep riprap banks — feeding on crawfish and minnows during low light hours or windy days.

It's important to note that a small section of a long stretch of riprap may hold 70 percent of the fish. Isolated features, such as a transition zone where rock sizes change or gravel ends, an underwater point, a pile of boulders forming a knob at the base of the riprap, a creek channel that swings nearby, or wood that has gathered in an area are likely targets.

"When you catch a quality fish, note the depth at which it was holding," says Illinois smallmouth aficionado George Liddle Jr., who catches trophy smallmouth along Lake Michigan's riprap shores. "That's the first key to putting together a solid riprap pattern."

You can cover a riprap bank thoroughly by fishing it parallel, using the buddy system. Position the boat at a slight angle, with the rear of the boat closest to the shore. The front angler fan-casts parallel to deeper rocks while his partner combs the shallower edge.

Crankbaits — crawfish colors in spring and shad patterns during summer — allow you to cover a variety of depths more thoroughly. When the water temperature is between 50 and 60 degrees, try jerkbaits.

Soft plastics work well, especially crawfish-style worms and grubs rigged Texas style, with the sliding sinker pegged to the hook.

If the water is stained and the fish are shallow, try flipping jig-and-pork frogs along the face of the riprap. It's a natural presentation when bass are feeding on crawfish. However, go light on jig size to reduce snagging between rocks.

RIPRAP hot spots include: (1) where rocks end, (2) underwater point, (3) boulder knob, (4) creek channel and (5) wood cover.

over sandy, shallow flats. You'll see as many baitfish there as anywhere."

By better understanding where and how bass use rock-type habitat, anglers can learn to more efficiently fish it.

LURE CHOICES FOR ROCKY AREAS

The same lures that catch bass in weeds and wood work well around rocks, but there are some differences, says Texas pro Jay Yelas.

"One of the biggest advantages to fishing rocky areas is you can use a lure with an exposed hook, which is going to improve your catch ratio," he explains. "You'll still get snagged, but usually that's because the lure has caught in the cracks of the rocks, and that will happen with or without the hook exposed."

Here are Yelas' lure choices for various rock cover:

• *Gravel Flats* — Carolina or split shot rigs enable you to cover the water quickly and effectively, which is important because the bass are likely to be anywhere. Use soft plastic 4-inch worms, lizards, grubs and reapers. Smaller baits are more effective for spotted bass and smallmouth. During

the summer and into the fall, crankbaits, spinnerbaits and topwaters also are good.

• *Rocky Points* — Again, the Carolina rig is tough to beat for locating bass. Early in the season, work 10 feet or shallower until you find the depth bass are using. During summer, idle over the point and watch your electronics for schools of bait. Once you locate them, key on that depth.

• *Rockpiles, Boulders* — The bass are going to be on the shady side, so choose a lure that falls vertically or spirals on the drop, like jigs, grubs, soft jerkbaits and tube baits. Bright days call for pinpoint casting because the strike zone is very specific, even in deep water. Also, a double-tail spider jig rigged on a 3/8-ounce leadhead can be fished on the fall or swum over the cover. Simply wind it slowly over the bottom, occasionally allowing it to bounce off the rocks. That's a big fish tactic for summertime.

• *Deep Rocks* — The same spider jig on a 3/4-ounce or 1-ounce football jighead is good for dragging along deep or rocky ledges. The heavy weight allows it to sink quickly, and when hopped off the bottom, it bangs on the rocks and stirs up silt like a crawfish.

If fish are suspended or lethargic, jigging spoons and metal "blade" baits, like Heddon Sonars and Silver Buddys, are good.

LOOK FOR TRANSITIONS

Like they do weedline and timber edges, bass use changes in bottom composition when staging or moving. That edge may be where big rock ends and gravel begins, or where a riprap bank ends along a clay bottom. It can also be a simple change in rock color.

"Bass seem to prefer diversity over consistency," says Mangus. "A shale bank or a bottom strewn with boulders of the same size isn't nearly as good as one that changes often. The change can be as subtle as a bottom switching from gravel to clay."

The area can be even better if the habitat is mixed. For example, a rocky bottom with scattered wood, a sand flat with patches of weeds, or a pea gravel bottom with a few boulders afford bass multiple edges within the habitat. If you can see those changes, target your casts accordingly.

HARD BOTTOM FLATS

There are times when bass, especially smallmouth, move onto a relatively barren sandy, gravel or clay flat to feed on minnows and crawfish. The best flats are fairly large and slope gently toward a major dropoff.

It's a pattern many anglers overlook because of the apparent lack of cover, yet it's one that can be quite productive during spring and fall. All bass will use hard bottom flats for spawning, but smallmouth will use them year-round.

"It doesn't take a lot of cover to keep a smallmouth happy," explains Mangus. "A single boulder, a patch of gravel, or a small piece of wood will hold them, even in clear, shallow water."

Mangus keys on the big sand flats of natural

A SPIDER JIG hopped through the shady crevices of a rocky shoreline will produce strikes in sunny conditions.

lakes during spring, late fall and any low light conditions. In clear water, he searches for isolated weed patches or gravel areas on the sand flat.

"A small weed patch in the middle of a gravel or sand flat can hold a limit of fish," he adds. "You might find largemouth and smallmouth mixed together there, too."

Mangus uses his eyes to locate those dark spots on the flat and fishes a number of lures in areas he suspects bass are using.

During coldwater periods, blade baits, like the Silver Buddy or Bullet Blade, are good for covering the water quickly. A Carolina rig lizard, a tube jig and a spider jig are good most of the time, and a jerkbait is ideal for fishing over the tops of rocks or weed patches.

If the fish are aggressive, spinnerbaits and crankbaits are good choices.

"If you find smallmouth on a big flat, cover as much water as quickly as you can," suggests Mangus. "Smallmouth will scatter and roam from one rock, log or weed patch to another."

BASS LOVE BOULDERS

Although bass prefer small boulders, they will use big rocks if they offer the primary cover.

"Think structure first, then think of the cover," says Missouri pro Denny Brauer. "If a large rock sits on a point, a bend of a creek channel or relatively barren flat, then it's probably going to hold bass."

Another exception, says Mangus, is a big rock isolated in a weedbed.

"It creates a change in the cover," Mangus insists. "A rock like that can hold the biggest largemouth or smallmouth in the weedbed."

Massachusetts angler Bob Pastick says when water levels drop on natural lakes during summer's dog days, largemouth will pull out of the shallows to the first breakline.

"I begin searching that 10- to 15-foot depth, looking for large, isolated rocks in the bends or on the points of the dropoff," he explains. "That's a great pattern for midday hours when the sun gets high."

The reason is that bass will scatter across the break and flat during low light hours. On bright days, they pull tight to the big boulders, making them easier to target. He keys on the shallow side of the rock and casts to it with 1/2-ounce jigs tipped with plastic crawfish.

"I don't care how clear the water is, I use big jigs and heavy line," he insists. "You need the weight to feel for the rock, and because you're fishing offshore, you've got wind to contend with. You need the heavier line because the rocks are jagged and will damage the line. Besides, the fish don't care. Get the bait in one's face and he'll take it."

Pastick says boulders become very important during fall on lakes that also contain submerged weedbeds. As vegetation dies, bass leave it for deeper rocks.

Don't overlook large, offshore rocky formations that break the water's surface. They provide a bridge from the water world to the terrestrial world, attracting other life forms upon which bass and their forage feed. Examine each rocky island for bass-attracting substructure, such as sloping points, underwater shelves and other types of cover.

Fishing The Bluffs

Rocky bluffs — those steep, stone-face banks that embrace creek channels — can be highly productive for smallmouth and spotted bass during cold months and early spring.

"Most bluffs have undercuts and lips on the shallow side that will attract bass in the ambush mode," says Missouri pro Randy Blaukat. "Take the time to study exposed sections of bluffs to get an idea what they might look like beneath the water's surface."

To locate deeper fish, Blaukat adds, idle along the bluff and watch the depthfinder for abrupt rock outcroppings or suspended schools of bass, especially spotted bass that hang out on bluffs.

Blaukat likes bluff sections where the creek channel approaches the wall or where it leaves it. (Frequently, the downcurrent side produces best.) If the fish aren't shallow, he works jigging spoons vertically along the edge. During early spring, he casts white hair jigs with pork frogs, grubs or 4-inch worms.

"If the fish are shallow, try bouncing a spinnerbait or crankbait along the face of the wall, or pitching a jig-and-pig," he adds. "If the water is clear, you can produce some violent strikes with topwater lures, like the Zara Spook. Active fish will come a long way to hit the lure."

During the early prespawn, when bass suspend along rocky faces, jerkbaits can be the ticket. And when water temperatures are high, bass seek cooler areas along the shaded bluff banks, where they can be caught by using spring or winter tactics.

KEY ON BLUFFS where the channel swings nearby. Fish usually will be positioned where the channel comes into the bank and where it leaves the bluff face.

FISHING VERTICALLY is the best way to approach a bluff bank. Spotted bass often school just off the bluff, while individual bass seek out crevices and undercuts.

FISH CHUNK ROCK in early spring and late fall with a jig-and-pig combination.

WHAT TO CHUNK AT CHUNK ROCK

From fall through spring, these hard bottom areas are prime locations for all types of bass

AS WITH MANY terms in bass fishing's vernacular, the definition of "chunk rock" varies from one angler to the next. Such disparities are due to the scope of each angler's fishing experiences, the waters he has fished and even the angler's preferred fishing methods. Even so, most anglers agree that chunk rock, however you define it, is capable of producing heavy catches of largemouth, smallmouth and spotted bass.

"To me," says Ohioan Joe Thomas, a regular on the BASS circuit, "chunk rock is anything from riprap to natural, basketball-size boulders. My favorite chunk rock ranges from the size of a baseball to that of a softball. It has a lot of cracks and crevices for bass to hide, but the rocks aren't so big that you're constantly hanging up. Crankbaits and even jigs bounce through it pretty well."

According to Thomas, the type of rock isn't critical, but the bottom composition that holds the rocks, and taking into account the weather, can determine the quality of the fishing. In early spring, Thomas looks for chunk rock on red clay banks in impoundments that feature this combination. Red clay and chunk rock comprise ideal crawfish habitat, and crawfish are the first forage that bass target in the spring.

Chunk rock banks on the main lake and in the lower ends of large creek arms produce best for Thomas at this time. The banks typically drop into deep water at a 45 degree or steeper angle.

If the springtime water temperature is 52 degrees or warmer and wind is blowing on the bank, Thomas opts for a 3/8-ounce Storm Wiggle Wart crankbait in a crawfish pattern. This wide wobbling lure delivers a nearly vertical dive. It immediately digs into the rocks, provided the cast is tight to the bank. Bottom contact is crucial for triggering strikes. When retrieved

A JERKBAIT IS a reaction lure capable of effectively covering long stretches of rocky shoreline.

(Opposite Page) MARK KILE LOOKS for points and other structure formed by chunk rock, since these are high percentage hookup spots for bass.

Jay Yelas On Chunk Rock

Jay Yelas offers these additional tips on fishing chunk rock.

■ "Any point made up of chunk rock is likely to hold bass. Even a real subtle nub of a point along a rocky bank can hold a fish. If the rocks are big enough, a single, large boulder that juts out from the rocks can cast enough shade to make a bass feel right at home."

■ "A chunk rock bank combined with wood cover can be good. I've run into situations like that on tidal rivers, where a combination of rock and wood produced bigger fish. Anytime you've got a dock on a chunk rock bank, it's far more likely to hold bass than a similar bank that doesn't have a dock. The dock gives big bass the option of moving shallow on the rocks or hanging deep in the shade of the dock next to a planted brushpile."

■ "When shad are up spawning on the rocks, there's usually a real good early morning and late evening bite. A lot of times it's hard to catch bass on chunk rock on a sunny, bluebird day with a moving bait like a spinnerbait, especially if the water's clear. Now, if the water's real dirty and visibility is only a foot, though, you might have to go to a crankbait instead of a spinnerbait. They'll also bite all day under overcast, windy conditions."

■ "You can catch worm-fish off chunk rock, but I always try to catch the aggressive fish. Usually your bigger fish will come on spinnerbaits, topwater lures or crankbaits, especially if the shad are up on the rocks. But in the early spring, a jig-and-pig is hard to beat."

on the 12- to 14-pound green Stren used by Thomas, the Wiggle Wart dives about 7 feet, which Thomas believes in most instances is plenty for bass feeding on chunk rock banks.

"Wind puts a chop on the water and often creates a mudline," says Thomas. "These factors help draw bass tight to chunk rock banks and make the fish more aggressive. I use a slow to medium retrieve with a stop-and-go cadence. That imitates a crawfish skittering for cover. The bait bounces off a rock, you stop it, and the bass clobbers it."

Thomas has found that without wind, bass relating to chunk rock are not as aggressive. Under calm conditions, Thomas fares better with a 3/8-ounce brown jig tipped with a brown No. 11 Uncle Josh Pork Frog. He has had excellent results with rubber, silicone and hair dressings, and often embellishes the brown skirt with a few strands of orange.

When he fishes chunk rock in extremely clear water, which he finds on many TVA lakes, Thomas switches to jerkbaits, such as Rapala's suspending 4 3/4-inch Husky Jerk in a silver/black back pattern. This lure produces smallmouth, spotted and largemouth bass for Thomas in the spring and fall when the water temperature ranges between 50 and 60 degrees. He fishes the jerkbait on 12-pound green Stren, makes quartering casts to the bank and imparts a jerk-pause action that maintains a steady cadence.

WESTERN ROCKS

Chunk rock is common in western Canyon reservoirs fished by veteran Arizona pro Mark Kile. His favorite chunk rock is smooth, rounded river rock ranging from baseball size to watermelon size.

Because many of the reservoirs Kile fishes contain so much rock, it's hard for him to pinpoint bass in large areas of rocks. Instead, he looks for isolated patches of this cover, which increases his odds for contacting bass. He also looks for points and other structure formed by the rock, since these are high percentage spots for bass. Points leading into creeks and coves often provide bass with chunk rock cover from the deep water on the end of the point to the shallows in the back of the cove.

This isn't to say Kile ignores long, straight stretches of chunk rock banks. At times he'll put his trolling motor on high and

JOE THOMAS USES a big jerkbait when fishing chunk rock in extremely clear water.

parallel a straight rocky bank with a buzzbait, jerkbait or crankbait and pick off bass scattered along the cover.

Kile keys on chunk rock during the spring and summer. In the fall, he believes bass spend most of their time roaming around after schools of shad in open water, which makes chunk rock less productive.

"Most people only fish visible chunk rock on the bank," says Kile, "but it also exists under water. I often fish it as deep as 20 feet on impoundments like Roosevelt Lake. I use my graph to find hard bottom areas, and then I feel the bottom with a 1-ounce football head jig for clusters of chunk rock that may be only as big as a car."

Kile matches the heavy jig with a spider grub and 20-pound-test line. He may bounce the jig quickly over the bottom or drag it with his trolling motor. Either way, there's no mistaking when the heavy jig bangs into rock. The spider grub nicely mimics crawfish and coaxes strikes. Kile has seen times when aggressively ripping the jig off the bottom — working it almost as you would a jigging spoon — has sparked phenomenal action from bass.

VISIBLE ROCK

World champion Jay Yelas concentrates on visible shoreline chunk rock — anything from the size of a softball on up.

"Chunk rock is great bass cover all over the country," says Yelas. "Some lakes are full of it, while others have sparse amounts. A lot of lowland reservoirs in the Southeast have little rock besides riprap. Other lakes, like Table Rock and Lake of the Ozarks, are just full of natural chunk rock."

Yelas fishes chunk rock in the spring and fall. It yields few bass for him in the summertime, because most bass are then relating to deep or shallow flats, or to offshore dropoffs, where they feed on shad and other baitfish.

In winter through early spring, Yelas casts crawfish pattern crankbaits and jig-and-pig combinations to chunk rock for bass feeding on crawfish. He prefers plastic crankbaits, such as the shallow

running Berkley Frenzy, over more buoyant balsastyle baits.

"You don't want a lot of buoyancy in a crankbait when you're fishing rocks," says Yelas. "You want the bait to stay down and grind bottom."

Another prime time for chunk rock, according to Yelas, occurs late in the spring, when shad move up and spawn on the rocks. At this time he goes with crankbaits and uses his signature Berkley spinnerbait in 1/2- and 5/8-ounce sizes sporting nickel tandem willowleaf blades, or a willow/Colorado combination with a white head and skirt. He always rigs his spinnerbait with a trailer hook when fishing chunk rock, since snagging on this cover is rarely a problem. Buzzbaits and walking-type stickbaits are also high priority chunk rock lures for Yelas.

"The shad usually spawn on main lake rocks," says Yelas. "This isn't the time to be fishing the backs of pockets or creeks. When I'm fishing a spinnerbait, I'm usually letting it drop just out of sight."

Yelas has learned that chunk rock also holds quality bass in the fall, when low water leaves shallow wood cover high and dry. Shad swarm to chunk rock to eat the algae, which has grown thick on the rocks over the summer.

"One of the tell-tale signs of good chunk rock fishing," says Yelas, "is when you throw a spinnerbait up on the rocks and big shad nip at the blades all the way back to the boat. When you run into that situation, there's going to be bass around."

A quartering cast to chunk rock banks produces well for Yelas, though there are times when he moves close and parallels the rocks, especially when fishing topwater lures. He finds the best topwater fishing takes place in the fall.

WITH BASS ALREADY attracted to rock, areas offering the added bonus of wood cover increase the potential for hookups.

BREAKING DOWN DAMS

Not only does a dam hold back water, it often holds big schools of bass

SOMETIMES BASS ANGLERS are too sophisticated for their own good. They pore over topo maps, hunting neglected humps and ridges. And in so doing, they may bypass the forest to get to the trees.

For sometimes, the best place to fish on a reservoir or river system is the most obvious place, the biggest slice of structure of them all: the dam.

Looming high above the water's surface, this concrete wall and its accompanying structures can be the closest thing to a sure bet when it comes to catching quality bass. As you will learn, these concrete blockades can be productive man-made bass attractors.

ROCKPILES AND OTHER inconspicuous submerged structure are prime areas for catching bass below dams.

TOURNAMENT TACTICS

Pro Charlie Ingram grew up fishing the Tennessee River and its many locks and dams, making him a crackerjack concrete expert.

"I especially like to fish close to the dam when the water in the reservoir is rising rapidly," Ingram says. "Heavy rains may send a rush of muddy water down the lake, and since the dam area is usually the deepest and clearest, that's where I'll head."

Ingram's boat is most often found near a dam in the early spring, although he says the area is good year-round for bass fishing.

When the lake rises, Ingram concentrates on riprap adjacent to the dam, which he calls "amazing structure." Ingram believes riprap is all too often ignored by otherwise knowledgeable Bassmasters.

"It's usually viewed as a catfish paradise, or simply too obvious a structure to be relied upon, but it can produce quality bass with consistency."

The keys to understanding riprap are several. Ingram believes its heat-absorbing qualities make it pay off in the early spring.

"On a calm, sunny day, the riprap will absorb solar energy and warm the surrounding water a few degrees, which can draw in baitfish by the millions," he says. "This is a superpattern for lunker bass in late February or early March. The fish find a combination of warmer water and concentrated forage."

As the water warms in late spring, Ingram finds that algae starts enveloping the piled-up rock, again attracting baitfish.

"Shad and fish fry feed on the algae," he explains. "Plus, decaying organic material is trapped in the cracks between the rocks, serving as a good food source for crawfish. To a bass, the riprap is like a buffet."

In rising water, bass may move very shallow on the riprap, but when the water falls or is stable, they'll be deeper. This is another reason Ingram likes to fish riprap — it provides a wide variation in water depth in a concentrated area. The fish don't have to swim long distances to find deeper or shallower water. He expects to find bass shallow on riprap in high water, when waves pound the structure and when heavy current is present.

Ingram feels most anglers err when choosing a lure to probe this broken rock.

"A deep diving crankbait is the most common choice, but it can lead to trouble," he says. "That big lip may get hung up in the broken rocks. Plus, how many times have you repeatedly cast a deep diver, only to get a strike and have the bass pop your line? When your lure constantly roots in riprap, line fraying is inevitable."

Ingram's favorite riprap lure in cold, clear water is a pearl-colored leadhead grub, which he feels imitates a shad.

"A grub will stay constantly hung up unless you *feel* it to the bottom, then immediately swim or pop the lure once you feel the line go slack," he advises. "But even if you do hang up, grubs are cheap. It's often quicker to bust off and retie than try to free the bait."

A LIPLESS CRANKBAIT imitates shad, the primary forage available to bass found below dams.

ALTHOUGH FISHING below dams can become crowded when bass are actively feeding, there are generally plenty of fish to go around.

Once the water warms above 62 degrees in spring, Ingram switches to a shallow running crankbait or a spinnerbait. He'll parallel the riprap in the 6-foot zone. He's also an avid night fisherman, and he finds the dam holds big fish surprises after dark in hot weather. "The fish hold deep during the day, but they'll move extremely shallow on the riprap at night and really hammer a spinnerbait," he says.

HACKER'S HINTS

Pickwick Lake guide Steve Hacker also spends considerable time probing around dams. He fishes Pickwick's headwaters below Wilson Dam and the extreme lower end of the lake, above Pickwick Dam. But rather than concentrating on the dam itself, Hacker moves to the first cove above the dam when fishing the lower end.

"Regardless of the reservoir you're fishing, the first creek or cove usually is a big one, and may hold a marina or launch ramp," he says. "The points at the mouth of this cove are especially good for big bass." Fishing one such cove on Pickwick, Hacker once caught five bass weighing close to 26 pounds, and then returned shortly thereafter to boat eight weighing 37 pounds.

"Most bass fishermen totally

Wing Dam Bass

Wing dams, or jetties, are found on every major river system and can provide excellent bass-holding structure when current is present. The wing dams are made from wood pilings and stacked rock formations, and they are designed to protect shorelines from siltation and erosion.

Baitfish and crawfish will congregate on the downcurrent side, attracting schools of bass. The structure can be fished by positioning the boat slightly downstream from the end of a jetty, casting crankbaits and spinnerbaits into the current and bringing them with the natural flow. Or, align the boat parallel to the wing dam and cast along the down current edge. Also, look for slack-water areas closer to shore, where bait and bass may congregate.

Watch for substructure, such as points or brushpiles that may have formed on the backside of the jetty. One small area could be home for a limit of bass.

Jerkbaits, buzzbaits and lipless crankbaits are other lure choices for fishing the jetties.

ROCK RUBBLE LEFT behind after the construction of a dam forms trash piles that provide current breaks for bass in swift water.

ignore these points," Hacker believes. "The launch ramp or marina closest to the dam is a favorite tournament takeoff point on most lakes, and eager competitors roar right past these points. They're a perfect access from deep water. The fact that many bass are released in this cove following tournaments is another reason to fish them."

Three things will dictate Hacker's lure and presentation choice: "Current, current and current!" He says if current is substantial and baitfish are present, he'll fish a deep diving crankbait, combing the points quickly for fish. If no current is there, he'll slow down and fish a hair jig, usually in white to match baitfish forage.

If these points don't produce, he hunts "switchbacks" both above and below the dam. "These are places where heavy current causes the water to flow in opposite directions. Bass will often be in the 'crease,' or dividing line, between the two current flows, or holding in eddies off to the side."

When the water is fast, Hacker relies upon a hair jig with no pork trailer. "A trailer will slow the fall and the lure will get swept away in the current," he explains.

Another unusual structural element Hacker fishes is the trash pile that sometimes accumulates in front of the dam after heavy rains. "Leaves, logs and other debris will form a floating mass that can hold a surprising number of bass, especially largemouth," he notes. "Use a jig and drop it down through the debris."

NOT ALL COVER is visible, and some of the best can only be located using electronics.

Dam Elements

When gazing in awe at a dam, it's easy to forget that this monolithic structure can be dissected into several elements, each providing a distinct habitat for bass. Among them:

■ **The Dam Wall** — This holds and stores water behind the dam and regulates water flow into the tailwater. The storage area is referred to as the "forebay" by hydropower engineers. Water is released through a "penstock," or power intake, then directed to a turbine-driven generator below the dam. The dam wall may have concrete shelves and ledges that can draw baitfish and bass.

■ **Riprap** — This is the broken rock used to shore up the earthen mound close to the dam, which was piled high when the dam was under construction.

■ **Perpendicular Walls** — Structures that direct watercraft into locks, or serve to direct the water's flow as it is released from the turbines, often run at right angles to the dam wall. These provide current breaks and eddies.

■ **River Channel Structure** — The river channel runs into the dam, providing a varied menu of structure for the Bassmaster, including ledges, stumps and submerged timber.

■ **Irregular Bottom Conditions** — While the dam was under construction, holes were dug, rock and earth moved and rubble piled up. These remnants of construction provide holes, mounds and other bottom irregularities close to the dam.

■ **Current** — Current can be viewed as a structure, in that it can attract and concentrate bass and forage. And nowhere on the lake are the effects of current so visible as they are around the dam. Current has an energizing effect on fish; when it turns on, so do the bass.

■ **Other Structure** — Sometimes barges pile up and lie idle for weeks close to a dam. These can provide shade and cover for bass. Peripheral structure such as storage tanks, pilings, and other fixtures commonly associated with dams can also be used by bass.

JACK'S FACTS

Tennessee guide Jack Christian fishes dams for less obvious reasons. "Perhaps the most overlooked area around the dam is the dam wall itself," he comments. "It appears to be straight up and down, but often it's slanted and has shelves and ledges beneath the water.

"Algae grows all over these. If you look down into the water, you can see schools of shad cruising back and forth along the dam. You'll also spot a large number of bluegill, too; both are great bass forage."

Christian parallels these concrete structures with a tailspinner lure, like a Little George, a metal blade bait, like the Silver Buddy, or a Rat-L-Trap.

"Try to knock the lure right against the wall, scraping it as you retrieve," he says. "Often, there's heavy current sweeping the wall and the bass won't move far to grab

CURRENT BREAKS FORMED by riprap and boulders are key areas below dams. The fish will hold in the slack water and ambush prey swept by in the current.

the lure. Your bait may come back with algae all over it, but you may come back with a big bass on your next cast."

Christian believes heavy current washes food particles out from between cracks in the rocks and sends tiny bits of algae floating off the walls, triggering a forage and predator movement."

Besides bass, Christian catches giant stripers and hybrids on dam structure during heavy current flow.

"If the fish aren't on the wall, I'll switch to a heavy spoon and make long casts into the current boils. This is where big stripers often hold," he relates.

Few anglers are aware of the many holes and rockpiles that often can be found immediately above or below a dam.

"When a dam is under construction, there's a monumental movement of earth and rock, and the resulting holes and mounds will really concentrate bass," he says. In slack water, he relies on a plastic worm or deep diving crankbait, but in current, he'll fish the shallower parts of these structures with a grub.

Christian believes many bassers ignore dams because they're not very scenic.

"They're big, ugly and industrial-looking, the farthest thing imaginable from a weedbed or other more picturesque bass structure," he reasons. "But they can hold bass just the same." Besides the areas mentioned, Bassmasters are urged to check out storage tanks, pilings where barges tie up, and idle barges themselves. "Bass often suspend beneath a stack of barges, just as they would under a bed of lily pads in a natural lake. Fish a grub or plastic worm close to the barge."

BECAUSE BASS ARE opportunistic feeders, dams are natural places for them to be, since they feature moving water.

Safety Notes

Warning: FISHING AROUND A DAM CAN BE HAZARDOUS TO YOUR HEALTH. Remember:
√ Obey all warning signs and signals.
√ Never enter posted areas.
√ Give wide berth to barges and other navigational traffic.
√ Always wear a life jacket when fishing around a dam.
√ Be especially cautious below the dam, where a sudden discharge of water can be extremely dangerous.
√ Sometimes (but not always), a warning siren or horn is sounded prior to the discharge; both boaters and bank fishermen should move away from the discharge area and prepare for rapidly rising water and greatly increased current.

DEEP STRUCTURE

While the crowds
are beating the banks,
venture offshore,
where the fishing is unspoiled . . .

RAY SEDGWICK identifies structure as a change in depth that provides bass a place to hide while awaiting prey.

STRUCTURE FISHING WITH THE PROS
Two deep water experts share their structure secrets

ABOUT 10 A.M. on a bright, sunny February day not long ago on West Point Lake, Ga., bass pro Bobby Padgett and a friend found a school of bass that defies the imagination. Studying his depthfinder, Padgett saw something on the bottom in 25 feet of water — he wasn't even sure they were fish, much less bass — and dropped a Hopkins spoon to investigate.

That first drop produced a 3 1/2-pound largemouth, and immediately Padgett knew they were on to something. Late that afternoon, 160 fish later, they finally called it a day. During the entire time, they never moved their boat more than 30 yards.

On a slightly different note, fellow BASS pro Ray Sedgwick has tagged well over 2,000 bass he's caught in the famous Santee Cooper Lakes (Marion and Moultrie) in South Carolina, where he lives.

Among his experiences over the years: He's caught as many as 20 fish at a time from a single stump. He has pulled the same tagged fish from the same stump four times over a two year period. And he once caught the same fish twice on the same structure six years apart.

What do these two anglers have in common? Both are among the most experienced and knowledgeable structure fishermen on the CITGO Bassmaster Tournament Trail. Padgett won the 1996 Alabama Invitational on Lake Eufaula, while Sedgwick won the 1995 Top 100 on Lake Seminole.

In the question-and-answer article that follows, Padgett and Sedgwick reveal some of their secrets.

In your opinion, what exactly is the definition of "structure"?
PADGETT: "To me, structure is anything deeper than 5 feet, which we cannot see, and which relates to the bottom contour. I believe structure basically refers to depth changes caused by ditches, channels and humps."

(Opposite Page) STRUCTURE CAN mean anything as imposing as a bridge or as subtle as a piece of driftwood. Knowing when to target both large and small structure is a key to patterning the bass.

THE SHARPLY defined contour of a deep breakline is the type of structure especially suited for a blade bait.

THE MOUTHS of major tributaries with points falling directly into the main river channel are key structure during the summertime, according to Bobby Padgett.

SEDGWICK: "I consider structure to be anything a bass can relate to in order to hide and ambush prey. At Santee, a bottom contour change of a single foot can be important structure, simply because they are essentially flat lakes without much of a contour change."

What's the biggest problem anglers have fishing structure?

PADGETT: "Anglers fish places, not fish. I fish (for) the fish I see on my depthfinders. To be a successful structure fisherman — to be able to effectively fish those places you can't see from above the surface — you absolutely have to become a good 'electronic fisherman.' Right now, very few anglers are good at this."

Is there a shortcut to successful structure fishing?

PADGETT: "In my experience, all the places where bass locate will have two or three good features, not just one. Naturally, the more good features, the better. For example, the outside of a channel bend will often hold fish. If there's a rockpile

on that bend, it's more likely to hold fish. If there is standing timber around the rocks, it's even better. These are things you have to learn to look for."

SEDGWICK: "When I go into a new area, I look at my depthfinder and also at the shoreline, because the shoreline can give strong clues to what's on the bottom. For instance, shoreline points nearly always extend out under the water, and the types and formations of trees on the shore can tell you the type of bottom. Just noticing something as simple as this can save you a lot of time."

Both of you pay a lot of attention to bottom composition. Why?

SEDGWICK: "Clay is nearly always better than anything else. It isn't really smooth — it's often full of holes — and this irregularity helps attract baitfish. I think this is also why sunken roadbeds are so productive."

PADGETT: "I agree. A hard bottom is always better. On West Point, I like pea gravel up to baseball-size rocks. Fifteen of my best 25 places there have this type bottom. One year when the water level on West Point dropped 20 feet, I went out to see just what made these places so consistently good, and the common denominator I found was the hard, gravel bottom. Now I always pay attention to the bottom wherever I'm fishing."

How do you determine bottom composition when you can't see it?

SEDGWICK: "Sometimes you can tell with a good depthfinder, but the most reliable way is by fishing. Toss out a bottom-hugging lure and drag it around and see what it feels like. Again, looking at the shoreline will also help."

Where do you start when you know you're going to fish structure? What is the very first step?

PADGETT: "Buy a good Corps of Engineers map or U.S. Geological Survey map and study it. Look for something in the depth you want to fish, such as 20 feet. But also look down as deep as 30 feet, simply because a lot of maps will be inaccurate by 8 to 10 feet."

SEDGWICK: "My key depth is 15 feet or less, year-round, anywhere, but exactly where in that range depends on the current conditions at that lake. Local information can be valuable, too. Don't ask someone where to fish on a lake, ask them how deep the fish are."

Are there any other ways to determine a starting depth?

PADGETT: "Sometimes you can put your boat on slow plane and study your depthfinder as you crisscross a deep cove. If you notice baitfish showing up consistently at a certain depth, this can be a basic starting point. But you don't want to use up a lot of time haphazardly looking for baitfish when you could be studying a specific area you've already found on a map."

Let's say we have determined we're going to fish a depth range of between 10 and 20 feet. Now what do we do?

PADGETT: "You study the map according to the time of year, using certain parameters of established fish behavior patterns to tell you where the bass might be. For example, in late fall and winter,

bass will be on the sunny sides of structure like channels and points."

Can you break it down more precisely?

PADGETT: "It varies slightly on different types of lakes, but in fall, for example, as bass start following bait, they may move several places. They may move up on secondary structure like shallow river channel bars in 5 to 8 feet of water; they may move back into the creeks; or if you're fishing a lake with a lot of points, the bass may migrate into coves near ditches and points."

SEDGWICK: "On any of these places, baitfish will be one of your main keys, and this is something every structure fisherman has to learn to do: Look for and be able to identify baitfish on a depthfinder. Actual bottom depth is not that important; it is a depth change that will attract the bait and the bass."

What happens in winter as the water gets colder?

PADGETT: "I suggest looking at the mouths of major tributaries that have points falling directly into the main river channel. The colder the water, the tighter to the bottom the bass will be, maybe even resting with their bellies on bottom. But under bright skies, the fish tend to move on top of the structure (in this case, the point) while on cloudy days the bass stay along the sides or edges of the structure."

Can you fish structure in the spring?

SEDGWICK: "Absolutely. If the water

BOBBY PADGETT uses a paper chart recorder to identify productive dropoffs and determine if bass and baitfish are present.

RAY SEDGWICK marks a wide area with marker buoys after finding it on a map. He then hones in on specific spots with the aid of his depthfinder.

temperature is in the 50s or lower, you fish much like you do in the winter, although perhaps not as deep. I think one of the most reliable places is along main channel breaks, where you have a steep drop from 3 or 4 feet down to 12 or 15 feet. Another place to look is where the mouth of a creek meets a main channel, or channel bends where a tributary or ditch flows in."

We often think of summer as a prime time for structure fishing. What do you suggest for that season?

PADGETT: "The easiest plan is to look for the biggest flat that drops off the fastest (steepest) into a channel. The fish you're going after moved up on that flat earlier in the spring to spawn, and they gradually will move away from it toward the first available deeper water. The steeper the drop, the less distance the fish will move."

Let's say you're going to fish a point falling into a river channel. How, exactly, do you start?

SEDGWICK: "Start by zigzagging back and forth over the point and the edge of the channel while you study your depthfinder. You want to get a feel for what it looks like, how hard it comes up, and how hard it falls down into the channel. You're also looking for any sign of baitfish or possibly even bass.

"If you see anything of interest, drop a marker buoy on it. I'm amazed at how few fishermen ever use buoys, but I may put out four or five to mark drops or fish."

PADGETT: "You never really know what's going to happen until you start fishing. Remem-

ber, when bass are on top of the structure, it's likely they are feeding. The lower on the sides they are, the less likely they'll be feeding. After you mark a place, drop a spoon down and jig it a few times, or throw out a jig, a plastic worm or even a crankbait. Just go fishing and see what happens."

Suppose you don't see any fish on your depthfinder. What do you do then?

PADGETT: "If the area really looks good with strong contour breaks and a hard bottom, I'll probably fish it anyway, although not necessarily as long as I will if I actually see fish. This is especially true if fishing on that lake is generally tough. When the fishing is really good, I won't stop to fish until I do see activity on the electronics. You nearly always see bass if you're really going to catch them."

What types of lures should a structure fisherman be able to use, and is lure selection really that important?

SEDGWICK: "Lure selection is important in structure fishing for the same reasons it's important in shallow water: You want to be able to cover the water efficiently, and you need to have confidence in whatever lure you're using.

"If you're fishing water no deeper than 18 or 20 feet and you've spotted bass on top of the structure, your best choice is probably a crankbait. You can cover the area quickly with a crankbait, and if bass are in a feeding mood, they'll hit it. In deeper water, I suggest a spoon, which can be worked fairly quickly and which bass will definitely hit.

"When bass are along the side of a point or breakline, a Carolina rig is often better, since it will cover the bottom at a slower speed. If the fish are suspended, a crankbait or perhaps one of Bobby's 1/2-ounce white deerhair jigs (Preacher Jigs by Mann's Bait Co.) can be used. Sometimes you can slow roll a spinnerbait over a drop if the structure isn't that deep."

PADGETT: "If bass are on the side of structure and not feeding, I may return to the spot three or four times during a day. This is another important element of structure fishing. Just because you don't catch anything in a spot does not always mean it's a bad choice.

"Structure fishing is all about timing. When bass are shallow, they're basically feeding, but when they're deeper, you either have to trick them into feeding, or wait for them to start feeding."

How do you trick a bass into feeding?

PADGETT: "Imagine yourself on a conveyor belt moving 5 mph. The fastest you can run is 4 mph, and there's a bear at the end of the conveyor belt waiting to eat you. All he has to do is wait, because sooner or later he's going to get you.

"Well, the bass is the bear at the end of the conveyor belt. Sooner or later it's going to get the shad that come his way. You have to put a lure down to where the fish is waiting and make it look like an easy meal. That's why vertically jigging spoons or fishing a deerhair jig is such an effective technique in colder weather. They look like a helpless shad fluttering down in front of the bass.

"When one fish eats, the others around it suddenly get very interested and start looking for other shad."

If either of you could summarize deeper structure fishing, what would you say?

PADGETT: "It's frequently a feast-or-famine situation, and that's probably what discourages anglers the most. Once you sample the feast, however, and see the whole picture come together, you'll generally want to do more of it."

SEDGWICK: "Structure fishing takes time and experience, and it isn't often that a fisherman goes out on a lake he's never seen before and hits the mother lode in deep water. It does happen, of course, but I think the place to really learn the basics of structure fishing is on a lake you fish often and have learned pretty well. Personal confidence and knowing how to use a depthfinder are critical."

Top 10 Deep Water Hot Spots

■ **Outside channel bends** — Underwater channels serve as highways for bass, and resting points are on the outside bends. Here, the water is deeper and the sides are steeper, providing easy access between deep and shallow zones.

■ **Rockpiles** — Especially important in Northern natural lakes and highland reservoirs everywhere, rocks are magnets for smallmouth. Fish them with bottom bumping lures like jigs and grubs.

■ **Sunken roadbeds** — Good topo maps show roadbeds as red dotted lines. Well-defined roadbeds show up clearly on depthfinders. Fish ditches as well as the roadbed itself, and concentrate on bridges.

■ **Points** — After determining the primary depth zone bass are holding, focus on points at this depth. Be sure to fish the sides of points as well. If a point drops off abruptly at the end — a "bluff point" — you've found a dynamite hot spot.

■ **Dropoffs/ledges** — Scour creek and river channels for sharp drops. Any extra cover, including stumps, brush and logjams, concentrate bass along a ledge.

■ **River bars** — Sandbars that form in rivers and the headwaters of reservoirs are especially good when they're washed by current. Dredge them with Carolina rigged lures, including small worms, pulled in the direction of the current.

■ **Ditches** — These shallow channels may or may not show up on topographical maps, so they're a subtle form of cover that other anglers might not know about. Keep an eye on your depthfinder as you motor across flats, and mark the spots where the bottom dips sharply.

■ **Humps** — Underwater islands and mounds are key structures whenever bass are deep. The presence of wood, grass or rock cover makes a hump even better.

■ **Stumps/timber** — Bass like objects, especially objects on a change in bottom contour. Find ledges, points and flats containing this wood cover and fish it with deep diving crankbaits and slow rolled spinnerbaits.

■ **Brushpiles** — Bass anglers and some state agencies make their own fish attractors by sinking brush and treetops over good structure spots, especially points. Search for them with your depthfinder along, and at the ends of points, and fish them with Texas rigged worms and jigs.

BECAUSE OF their irregular shape, ledges are transitional areas that hold fish, making them prime spots for catching bass most of the year.

FISHING ON THE EDGE

To find bigger bass, learn to locate and fish the hot dropoffs

IN THE LIQUID WORLD, bass behavior is controlled by countless "edges." These boundaries can be as obvious as the shoreline itself or as subtle as the undulating sway of a grassline.

On these edges, unseen depth changes (created by rock or other submerged topography) form ledges that control fish movements no matter where a bass calls home. Although the depth range and the techniques required may change from region to region, their importance to bass fishermen does not.

Whether it's called a ledge or a dropoff, the words describe the same thing: a perceptible change in the bottom contour. However, the depth change needed for a significant ledge in one part of the country may be quite different somewhere else.

For instance, a Texan like CITGO Bassmaster Classic qualifier Alton Jones might consider a ledge that tops out at 10 feet and drops sharply to 20 to be a major break on one of his home lakes. The same ledge on a California impoundment fished by Robert Lee, perennial winner of California BASS tournaments, might not garner a second glance. Put this same ledge underneath veteran pro, Tom Mann Jr., who lives near and fishes Georgia's Lake Lanier, and you could have a third opinion on the subject.

However, while the depth of ledges can vary dramatically, these three pros all agree on one thing: The severity or sharpness of the drop is the common characteristic of a productive ledge. The sharper, the better.

But what makes one ledge more productive than the next? Often, it means a steep break that rises up to a flat top with some sort of rock or wood cover to hold fish along the edge. It doesn't matter if the ledge is formed by a main feeder creek intersecting the river channel or by a sharp drop on the inside bend of a creek channel. What makes a difference is the existence of key, fish-holding areas.

The object is to find irregularities (or "sweet spots," as Jones calls them) along the ledge, just as you would do in evaluating visible clues along a shoreline. These key zones come in various forms, including points, pockets, high spots, steeper sections, rockslides, boulders, stumps and other changes that distinguish one area of the drop from the rest.

The basic procedure for inspecting ledges is simple: Move from deep to shallow in a zigzag pattern to locate channel bends or breaks and the sweet spots they hold.

(Opposite Page) THE SEVERITY or sharpness of a dropoff is the common feature of a productive ledge. These sharply defined areas are most prominent in Western impoundments.

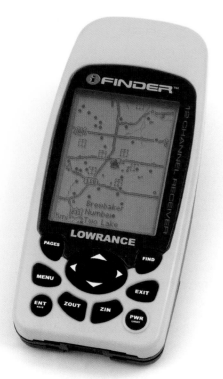

ONCE YOU'VE FOUND a productive section of a ledge, you'll want to go back again and again. GPS units are invaluable in getting you back to the good spots.

A JIG-AND-PORK COMBINATION is an excellent choice when cast to a ledge and worked slowly down the drop or fished parallel to the edge.

In part, the search for a productive ledge pattern begins with water clarity. In clear water, ledges are more important and generally need to be deeper and sharper than ones found in stained conditions. While muddy or severely stained water usually doesn't extend down to deeper ledges, ledge fishermen most always benefit from clear water.

Once a ledge is found, it is then vitally important to spend some time scanning the area with sonar. The goal here is to find any irregularity that might hold fish.

Another key element of ledges is the amount of cover present. While an abundance of cover has the capability of holding a larger number of bass, it is often easier to catch fish from isolated cover.

This philosophy goes back to the basic goal of bass fishing, which is being able to accurately predict the position of fish and consistently present a bait to them. Although isolated cover might hold fewer fish, a fisherman will know exactly where they are located.

In general, cover tends to keep fish shallow. Without it, fish have no option but to move deeper. The more cover available to bass, the more willing they are to move shallow and roam away from the edge of the drop. As fish become less aggressive or more finicky, they will hold tighter to the very edge of the break. When bass shift into a neutral or negative mood, they will either slide down into deeper water or suspend just off the structure.

Like other bass fishing situations, bait plays an important role in how bass are positioned on ledges and breaks. Fishermen experienced in sonar use can actually gauge the feeding tempo by observing the position of the bait on structure. For instance, tightly grouped schools of bait located just behind the edge of a drop can signal a prime feeding opportunity.

While bait can alert anglers to bass activity, it can also change the playing field within a matter of hours. As the prey moves, so does the predator. So wherever bass stop to ambush their prey, that instantly becomes the new sweet spot. Although these constant adjustments may seem terribly confusing, the more an angler knows about what lies beneath the surface, the simpler it becomes. This is especially true whenever there are fewer or more isolated sweet spots on a ledge.

In most cases, ledges can be divided into one of two categories: those on the main body of water and those found in creeks.

Generally, main lake ledges are more pronounced, but because they offer countless combinations to choose from, it's impossible to describe every factor that makes an area productive. The ideal situation, however, is a ledge formed by the intersection of a major feeder creek with the main river channel.

In creek channel situations, a fisherman needs to look for the same attributes, even though the depth will be less and the sharpness of the ledge more subtle. The best creek ledges are formed where a small culvert or ditch intersects the creek or where inside or outside turns of the creek produce an abrupt dropoff.

Although ledges can be productive nearly year-round, seasonal preferences are often dictated by the type of lake being fished, an angler's confidence in those areas and the fishing methods one prefers.

In the spring, ledges that offer ready access to a spawning flat generally harbor a large population of bass. Once an angler pinpoints these areas, the next

"SWEET SPOTS" AND KEYS TO PRODUCTIVE LEDGES
1. High spots
2. Points
3. Stumps, laydowns
4. Isolated cover
5. Sharp, abrupt drop offers quick access to deeper water
6. Current
7. Rock slides
8. Pocket
9. Boulders
10. Flat

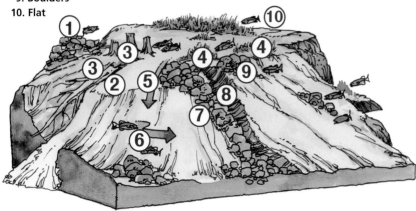

Top Lures For Ledges

■ **Jigs** — A 3/8- to 1/2-ounce jig-and-pig is an excellent choice when cast to the flat and worked slowly down the drop or fished parallel along the ledge. In sparse cover, the football head design (a longtime western favorite that is gaining converts across the country) imparts a lot of subtle action to the bait even at ultraslow retrieves.

■ **Spinnerbaits** — A slow rolled, 3/4- to 1-ounce spinnerbait is one of the best search lures for plying ledges from top to bottom. A No. 5 or No. 7 single willowleaf or Indiana blade is preferred, since these shapes allow the bait to sink faster and rise less on the retrieve than do Colorado models. With the sometimes-overlooked Indiana version, an angler gets a similar amount of vibration without as much drag as the Colorado style.

■ **Crankbaits** — Great coverage baits and documented producers, crankbaits are particularly effective when bass are aggressive. However, to be productive, cranks need to at least "tick" the cover or structure being fished. That means using a lure that dives deeper than the lip of the ledge (which precludes them for use on some of the deeper drops commonly found in the West).

■ **Plastic Worms** — Like jigs, plastic worms are effective in targeting key areas on a ledge. They become even more important as bass position themselves in various depth ranges. Worm sizes can vary from 8- or 10-inch models like Zoom's Old Monster ribbontail (which Tom Mann Jr. prefers) to a 5-inch Zipper worm (gaining popularity among western fishermen like Robert Lee). Carolina rigged plastics also find some use in these conditions, primarily when the fish are on top of the ledges.

step is to find small ditches that lead from the creek channel to the bank. In the prespawn period, it's usually a matter of fishing the bank within a couple hundred yards of where the ditch meets the shoreline. In postspawn, the fish are often on the creek channel ledge itself.

"Bass will roam away from these ledges more in the spring than at any other time of the year," remarks Jones. "But if you're after really big fish, I rarely catch one that's not right on the edge of the drop."

Although Mann recognizes some of the opportunities available in spring, he feels that ledges are far more predictable and productive in summer, winter and fall.

"The best time to pattern ledge fish — to know they will be there for a prolonged period of time — is the dead of winter or middle of summer, when a lot more fish are in deep water," he notes.

For those who may not feel as confident on main lake ledges in summer, Jones and Lee recommend looking around primary points, humps and ridges closer to the main lake. In these situations, there is still a premium on learning an area, since each structure may contain various drops or ledges. Some are obvious and receive ample fishing pressure, while others may go unnoticed.

One item not to ignore when fishing ledges, especially in summer, is the presence of current. According to Mann, current has a tremendous effect in power generation lakes.

"When the water is moving, you are 10 times more likely to catch fish on drops because current pulls them back to the ledge and the cover. It's like the difference between night and day. So when they're pulling water, you want to be in one of your primary areas."

Clearly, learning how to fish ledges not only teaches an angler how to read a lake, but it helps him find areas that offer the greatest potential for truly memorable catches. Once he gains a certain comfort level in fishing these submerged bass pathways, the phrase "living on the edge" takes on a whole new meaning.

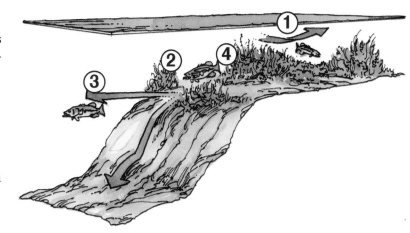

LEDGES AND BASS MOODS

1. The more cover available, the more willing bass are to roam away from the edge and move shallow.
2. Less aggressive or finicky bass hold tighter to the very edge of the break.
3. Neutral or negative feeders will suspend or move deeper.
4. Tightly grouped schools of bait just behind the ledge can signal a prime feeding opportunity.

SECONDARY POINTS shine especially in postspawn because the fish use them as rest stops en route to main lake points and deeper water.

SECONDARY POINTS: OVERLOOKED HOT SPOTS

From spring through fall, points inside coves can produce limit catches

IN ANY TOURNAMENT and during any weekend, bass can be caught from a variety of areas and on several patterns.

The most reliable patterns and the biggest fish, however, usually relate to subtle, overlooked areas. Since these spots can be hard to find, they typically receive little pressure from other anglers.

Secondary points — those jutting out from the bank inside coves and bays — are neither subtle nor hard to find, yet they are largely ignored by fishermen during the prime times of spring and fall.

"In spring, bass fishermen have a habit of sticking to the main lake points or the very backs of spawning coves," suggests pro angler Dean Rojas.

"They move very fast between those two areas, passing up the secondary points on their way back. That's too bad, because throughout the spawning cycle, fish moving in and out use these points as transition areas."

As bass move between deep water haunts and shallow nesting/feeding areas, they stop along the way at "staging areas," or collection points, where they can rest and await conditions favorable to further movement. Because bass, like big game animals, use the same routes throughout the seasons, the best secondary points hold fish during prespawn and postspawn and again in the fall. They literally become a swinging door between deep water and shallow flats.

IMPORTANT POINTS

While small coves and creeks may have only one or two secondary points in them, large basins and creeks have a dozen or more points leading back to shallow water. With bass on the move and so many secondary points to search, how does an angler determine which structures have the greatest potential for holding concentrations of staging fish?

"The location of the best secondary points depends on how far along the bass are in their migration," notes Rojas. Once you figure out where they are — on points closest to the main lake, in the backs of coves or somewhere in between — you can put a pattern together and duplicate it elsewhere on the lake.

Although numerous secondary points are found between the mouth and the back of a cove, only a few have the characteristics that will hold good numbers of staging fish.

"I always look for points where a deep channel or ditch runs close by," he explains. "The best point will have the channel sweeping right up against it. Also, I look for a point that has at least one side that has a steep drop or edge."

POINTS FOR SUMMER AND FALL

Texas angler Craig Schuff agrees with Rojas' assessment, and he adds that the better secondary points hold fish throughout most of the year. In summer, Schuff recommends anglers look for secondary points that touch relatively deep water.

A prime example is a secondary point formed by a creek channel swinging up against the bank, or one formed between a submerged oxbow and river channel.

"I have a favorite secondary point that I catch fish on every summer," Schuff notes. "The point separates two creek channels, each going bank to bank beyond the point. A spot like that can be good most of the year, especially when current is present."

In fall, the shallow water starts to cool, drawing hordes of bass and shad into the backs of creeks and coves. During this period, the secondary points at the front of the cove are again used as transition areas during the migration to the shallowest water.

However, the shallower secondary points at the back of a creek are typically used as ambush spots, where the bass herd shad on top of the points.

Some of the most productive secondary points during the fall migration are those created by a simple channel swing. Bass take advantage of

USE A CRANKBAIT to effectively work the sloping contour of a secondary point.

DEAN ROJAS works spinnerbaits across secondary points during the prespawn.

shad moving up on the warm, shallow flat of the point. As the creek or cove continues back, becoming almost a bank-to-bank channel, bass will even hold on the smallest points in wait for careless baitfish.

FINDING THE LESS OBVIOUS

Operating under the principle that less is more, Darryl Burkhardt of Oregon believes that finding less obvious structure is the key to finding numbers of quality fish.

"I believe the best secondary points are going to be the submerged (hidden) ones," confirms Burkhardt. "The greatest thing about these points is that they're overlooked, and so I always try to find them."

The problem is that submerged secondary points are obviously the toughest to find. Burkhardt begins his search with a detailed topographic map of the lake. "If you know how to read your topo map and know the water level of the reservoir," explains Burkhardt, "you can find those underwater points."

After he has identified the most promising hidden points, he uses a ruler to draw lines intersect-

DON'T OVERLOOK secondary points when they have important features like standing timber, which gives the fish all the more reason to use them.

ing features on the bank that should be easily visible once he's on the water. Burkhardt uses the previously identified features to triangulate the general area of the submerged point.

Once in the area, the Oregon angler uses his paper graph sonar to pinpoint the submerged structure.

It's important to carefully define the point's features, says Burkhardt, so he motors around the structure looking for a subtle feature such as a rockpile, brushpile or deep edge that will hold a concentration of fish. Then he tries to confirm whether fish are present.

"When prospecting for fish-holding features, I

use a split shot or Carolina rig," explains Burkhardt. "These rigs are like a depthfinder on the end of your arm — if you know the fall rate of the weight you're using, you can tell the depth by counting how many seconds it takes to reach bottom. And when you drag a Carolina rig or split shot worm, you can tell when you're pulling it over cover or dropping off a breakline."

SECONDARY POINTS are often completely submerged on lowland reservoirs, such as this one that is exposed during a drawdown.

SHALLOW HOT SPOTS

On lowland reservoirs, the better secondary points are often completely submerged — making them tough to find. They are typically flat and shallow, which makes them hard to locate with electronics. However, because they are tough to identify, they typically hold good numbers of fish.

"Shallow secondary points located below the waterline are difficult to find if you don't have the right equipment," adds Schuff. "I have found that liquid crystal depthfinders can't pick up the subtle clues to the point's existence." He says a flasher unit allows him to pick up a change as small as 1 foot, which can indicate the presence of a point in a lowland reservoir.

"When I am looking for these shallower secondary points," explains Schuff, "I keep my eye on my flasher at all times. I am usually fishing with a Rat-L-Trap or a spinnerbait in an effort to cover water as quickly as I can. That's the only practical way to find these overlooked structures."

Schuff warns that the key to locating a concentration of fish on these structures is to find that single, subtle feature. One of his favorite fish-holding features is a wash or erosion ditch. He explains that most secondary points have a ditch or wash that provides drainage during low water conditions.

"I have a textbook secondary point that fits this situation," he volunteers. "The point curves a bit and has a wash on one side. At the top of the wash is a stump with its roots exposed. I can fish that entire point and not get a strike — until I cast near that wash. And I almost always find a few fish holding next to that stump."

Follow the advice and lead of these top pro anglers and give secondary points a try. As Oregon's Burkhardt suggests, "Secondary points can be a lot of trouble to find. And it can be even tougher locating that subtle piece of cover that's holding the fish." But the rewards for your efforts are some great fish-holding structure that should produce limits throughout most of the year.

A Western Strategy

Former Westerner Dean Rojas approaches secondary points differently, depending on the season and the prevailing conditions.

"In early spring," adds the Texas transplant, "I prefer to work spinnerbaits and crankbaits when fishing for prespawn fish. However, water clarity basically dictates how I am going to approach a promising point. If the water clarity is real good, I slow down and fish small plastic baits."

During the postspawn period, Rojas switches over to a split shot or Carolina rig, fished between 10 and 25 feet deep. He typically begins by fishing the gut or channel leading out of the back of the cove and up to the secondary point. If the gut doesn't produce any fish, he turns to the secondary point itself.

"I typically begin casting to the shallower water of the small cove that is often formed by these features," explains Rojas. "If there are any shallow fish, those are the ones I want to catch first. My second effort will be directed to the top of the point itself. Finally, I position the boat so that I am casting and working my bait somewhat parallel to the breakline."

Rojas explains that once rested, postspawn bass will feed aggressively to replenish energy reserves used up during the spawn. Groups of postspawn fish will typically suspend at the end of the point, and if water clarity is good, they will move a great distance to take a bait.

Beginning in early summer, the midday topwater bite for which western impoundments are famous, kicks into high gear. As summer continues, ripping jerkbaits is an excellent way to draw up postspawn fish.

"In May and June," instructs Rojas, "you can use larger baits because the mature shad have moved into the coves and creeks to spawn. As fall approaches, I downsize my baits because the bass are foraging on the smaller young-of-year shad."

A HUMP IS ANY RISE in the lake bottom surrounded by deeper water — such as the stone wall exposed during a lake drawdown.

HOW TO FIND AND FISH HUMPS

These underwater high spots are bass magnets throughout summer

THE BLACK BASS is a very adaptable creature. It can live in a variety of waters and will consume a smorgasbord of forage.

But wherever they live and whatever they eat, all bass share one basic trait — they seek out areas where they can hunt and ambush their prey. And one of the best places to find their favorite foods — crawfish and baitfish — is on submerged humps, bumps and islands.

During the summer months, bass gravitate to these structures. They do so for food, of course, but bass experts also believe the bass use humps as sanctuaries from the hordes of anglers plugging along the bank. In many clear water

impoundments, humps can serve as cool oases away from hot, shallow water. Whatever the reason, humps make great fishing spots, especially in the heat of the summer.

"If I had to pick one time of year and one piece of structure to win a tournament, it would be in the summer on a hump," notes pro angler Alton Jones of Waco, Texas. That should be ample reason for you to learn to identify and locate these offshore hot spots.

WHAT ARE HUMPS?

Simply put, humps are bumps on the lake bottom. They come in all shapes, sizes and heights. Humps are even found in wide ranges of depth, from a few feet down to more than 100 feet. These bottom bumps provide bass with some unique contours to hide and feed around.

The best way to understand humps is to study the side of the road as you drive down the highway. Imagine the roadway is underwater. You can see how the roadway contours rise and drop off. Think how the bass would live near that rockpile at the exit ramp. The mound on the highway esplanade would also make a great ambush point. These same types of structure are under most flooded reservoirs.

Many of the reservoir humps are actually remnants of roads, stone walls and building foundations. These bass holding structures are often easy to locate on lake contour charts. An old geological survey map made before a reservoir was flooded can also point out bottom structures and humps.

Finding a secret lake hump is a real prize for most anglers. But not all humps hold bass. Some are completely devoid of life, while others are loaded with fish.

Jones looks for humps near these "bass highways." He says some of the best humps are found on the edges of reservoir creek channels. The bass use the channel edges as travel lanes to the shallow spawning areas. When the bass leave the spawning flats in late spring, they follow the channel edges out to deep water. Typically, these fish stop at the first hump they encounter in their travels.

In natural lakes where creek channels are nonexistent, anglers need to look for other, less obvious travel lanes. One of the biggest mistakes many bass anglers make is to fish around the first hump they find, says two time Classic qualifier Terry Baksay of Monroe, Conn. "Arbitrarily fishing humps will not necessarily produce fish," he says. "The hump must be associated with some feature extending from the bank to deep water."

He especially recommends humps on the edges of large weedbeds and off the tips of points.

FISHING HUMPS

There are four basic methods for fishing humps. But of all the techniques, crankbaiting outshines them all. Over the past decade, numerous summertime tournaments have been won by anglers working the offshore humps with crankbaits — and for good reason.

During the summer, bass in the southern impoundments feed heavily on shad. In the more northern natural lakes where shad cannot survive the cold winters, the alewife is the primary forage fish. Both baitfish species are "pelagic" fish that live out in the open water.

ALTON JONES prefers crankbaits for working humps because they maintain continuous contact with their tapering contour lines.

The Yankee Rig

Largemouth and smallmouth bass have a tendency to suspend over humps. When that happens, the fish become very difficult to catch. About the only way to entice them to bite is to hold your lure in front of their noses. Some ingenious anglers developed a rig to do just that — using the "drop shot rig," or, as it is affectionately known in the Northeast, the "Yankee Rig."

To the average bass angler, the Yankee Rig looks like a Carolina rig tied backward. To begin, tie a No. 1 or 1/0 hook to the line, leaving at least 2 feet of excess line beyond the hook knot. Slip a 1/8- to 1/4-ounce bullet weight or egg sinker on the tag end of the line. Then add a glass bead beneath the sinker and tie a swivel or split ring to the end of the line, from 1 to 2 feet below the hook.

"It's basically a modified flounder rig," said Terry Baksay, a professional tournament angler from Connecticut, where the Yankee Rig was perfected.

Flounder are very popular sportfish along the northeastern coastline, where anglers use special rigs featuring a weight on the bottom and a hook suspended 1 to 2 feet above the sinker. In the tide, the bottom weight keeps the bait out of the mud and away from crabs — and in the strike zone of the hungry flounder.

Most anglers finish the Yankee Rig with a small 4-inch plastic worm. This worm, suspended above the bullet weight, mimics the baitfish that swim around the humps. Baksay says he likes the Yankee Rig because it keeps the worm up where the bass can see it.

As you drift or drag the rig over a hump, the weight bounces along the bottom, clanging the bead against the weight to attract attention. Above the noisemakers, the worm wriggles enticingly to attract those finicky bass.

These fish follow the windblown plankton around the lake. As the wind pushes the plankton over the humps, the baitfish come dangerously close to the bass ambush areas. Bass anglers can capitalize on this bass-baitfish relationship by running a crankbait along the baitfish trail.

The key to crankbait fishing is to get a lure that dives deep enough to reach the top of the hump. You want the bait to maintain contact with the bottom throughout much of the retrieve, Jones explains. For the Texas pro, the crankbait is doing more than catching fish. It is also letting him know what the bottom is like.

"I always have a marker buoy up on the deck with me when I throw a crankbait," Jones says. "If I catch something, I kick the buoy over so I can cast again to the same spot."

Crankbait colors can play a significant role in an angler's summertime success. Because the fish are feeding on shad or alewives, more natural-looking baits come highly recommended. But most professional anglers change their crankbaits frequently during a tournament. They continually try to find the exact color and lure shape that bass will consistently strike.

For example, if you catch one fish on a shad-colored crankbait and repeated casts come up blank, that doesn't mean the hump is devoid of bass. A subtle change in crankbait color could produce another fish.

However, the crankbait bite can be short-lived. Once the active bass get caught, the crankbait repeatedly comes back empty. When that occurs, the Carolina rig becomes the hump angler's best weapon.

There is no magic in the Carolina rig, Baksay says. It's simply a "chuck-and-drag" style of fishing. Cast the Carolina rig out and slowly drag it back to the boat. It's just about that simple.

Carolina rigs for hump fishing do need some fine-tuning, mainly with the weight size and leader length. Vary the sinker weight depending on the hump's depth. On shallow water humps, Baksay

BIG CRANKBAITS worked across shallow humps make a lot of noise — and attract big smallmouth.

recommends smaller 1/4- to 1/2-ounce weights. A heavy weight can spook the bass if it splashes too hard on the water. On humps deeper than 10 feet, at least a 1-ounce weight is better.

The leader length is also key. On the shallow humps, those less than 6 feet deep, a short leader — say, 2 feet long — is often more productive than a longer one, Baksay says. Bass tend to hold closer to the bottom on the shallow humps. The shorter leader keeps the bait within the strike zone.

Bass periodically suspend off or above deeper humps, remarks Baksay. He ties Carolina rigs with longer 4- to 5-foot leaders. The longer leader prevents the bait from sinking too close to the bottom and out of the strike zone.

Most anglers hook soft plastic lizards on the business ends of their Carolina rigs. Baksay suggests the Lunker City Mud Dog, while Jones opts for the Lake Fork Ring Fry.

When the more active baits fail, Baksay and Jones both slow down on the humps. Jones goes for a Texas rigged Riverside worm. "Everybody is using the Carolina rig today, but the Texas rig is often overlooked," Jones says.

Baksay reaches for an oversize tube lure. "The tube is an ideal bait when the hump bite is slow," he says. "Drop the tube down to the bottom and bounce it around any subtle imperfection along the top of the hump. Stay alert. The fish tend to hit the tube on the fall. If the lure stops falling, set the hook."

FINAL THOUGHTS

Hump fishing requires an ability to read a depthfinder in order to pinpoint the bass feeding areas. Boat handling skills also come into play, as most humps are found in open water and near pleasure boat travel lanes. And an intimate knowledge of the shape of the hump can help you understand how the bass are relating to the structure.

SOME OF THE BEST humps are offshore and can only be located with a topographic map, meaning they are generally less pressured and hold more fish.

A HEAVY SPINNERBAIT is a top producer for bass buried in deep weedbeds.

DEEP WATER STRATEGIES FOR NATURAL LAKES

Try this pro's tips for catching big bass deep in natural lakes

PAUL CONVERSE uses his graph recorder for more than just following bottom contours. He relies on it for locating the thermocline, baitfish and structure, like rockpiles and stumps.

PAUL CONVERSE'S FIBERGLASS rod arced toward the water, and its guides creaked against the strain of unyielding, 20-pound braided line.

A 3-pound largemouth launched from the deep, clear water of the southern Michigan lake, then bolted recklessly through some weeds. Moments later, the Elkhart, Ind., policeman had the defiant bass cuffed by the lower lip.

"That's what I'm talking about," said Converse as he hoisted yet another quality bass into the boat. "These fish just don't see baits like they used to."

He was referring to the bass that reside in deep water on the Midwest's natural lakes. Converse believes deep tactics have become a lost art among today's anglers.

"Tournaments have put so much emphasis on finding and catching fish fast that anglers have forgotten how and where to find bass deep," he explains. "As a result, the fish living away from the shallows don't get as much pressure, and that's just fine with me."

Years ago, anglers recognized that the deep weed edges and rocky bottoms of clear water northern lakes harbor large schools of quality fish. But as tournaments gained popularity, fishermen began looking for faster and easier ways to get a limit. They turned to the shallows.

"Many of today's younger fishermen don't have the patience to fish deep," explains Converse, a top contender in the BASS club ranks. "There's no question that shallower fish can be easier, but with a little patience and the proper strategies, you can catch bigger bass in deeper water."

(Opposite Page)
BEFORE SHORELINE fishing took hold in modern bass fishing, fishing deep water was considered the only way to go. Today, while shorelines remain the top choice, the fishing remains hot offshore.

And that's not the only advantage. Deep fish are less affected by cold fronts and bright, bluebird days than are shallow fish.

"You have to slow down and scale down your lure size, but when conditions are tough the deeper fish tend to bite better than the shallow fish," says Converse.

The Hoosier angler believes so strongly in his approach

that he fishes deep patterns year-round, even during the spawning season, when most fish are shallow.

"I always check deep areas, because not all fish spawn at the same time," he insists. "I believe that under most conditions, 90 percent of the adult fish are going to be deep."

Especially after the spawn. Bass school on the deeper structure during summer, and they'll stay there until the waters cool in the fall.

"Winter also can provide excellent deep structure action," he says. "Bass really school then and you can have 100 fish days if you can bear the weather."

How deep is deep? That depends upon the lake. Depth is relative to the lake you're fishing. In a lake with a maximum depth of about 30 feet, deep water may be 9 to 15 feet. On another natural lake with 60 feet of water, Converse may key on depths from 15 to 25 feet.

"A good deep water lake also will be a good shallow water lake," he adds. "Lakes with a lot of big gravel and sand flats tend to support more bass than deep, bowl-shaped lakes with limited shallow water cover. The shallow flats support the food chain and provide optimum spawning habitat."

After the spawn, Converse probes the deep edges around those flats that have abundant vegetation and plentiful baitfish.

"Two things help me decide how deep to fish in the summer," he offers. "First, I use the thermocline to determine the absolute deepest the fish will be. Second, I study the clarity of the water and its effect on the depth at which the weeds grow."

The thermocline is a band of water at which the temperature and oxygen content changes drastically in a lake. Warmer waters with more oxygen lie above the thermocline while cold, dead water sits below it. Very few aquatic creatures can live below there.

You can locate the thermocline either with electronics or by monitoring baitfish schools in open water. It is indicated on a quality fish locator as a dark, horizontal band between the bottom and the lake's surface.

Converse will follow the thermocline toward the shoreline, looking for areas where it intersects with summer bass habitat. For example, if the thermocline appears at 20 feet, he'll idle toward points, humps or weedlines in water 15 to 20 feet deep. He then probes that structure for more irregular features or changes in bottom or cover. That's where the big bass are, he says.

Water clarity not only dictates how deep the weeds will grow, but how aggressive the bass may be. The clearer the water, the deeper the grass grows — because of light penetration. The outside edges of those weeds become highways that big bass use, and they become a focal point of Converse's search.

On the other hand, Converse believes bass in extremely clear water are more wary. They will lose their aggressiveness when boat shadows pass overhead.

"I don't mind fishing clear lakes, but I prefer a little color or wind to help camouflage my presence," he adds. "If it is clear and calm, you've got to sit a little farther off the structure and make longer casts."

Time of day can make a difference, too.

POINTS AND HUMPS are ideal summer hangouts for bass. To find the key areas in deep water, first determine the depth of the thermocline. Concentrate on areas where the thermocline level intersects structure — and where the baitfish are prominent. Here, a dropoff at the edge of a weedbed, located just above the thermocline and on the end of a point, holds the quality bass.

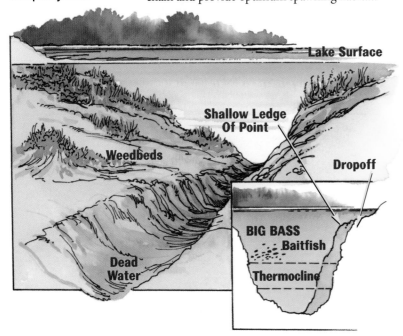

Lake Surface

Shallow Ledge
Of Point

Weedbeds

Dropoff

BIG BASS
Baitfish

Dead
Water

Thermocline

Converse says many anglers wait until the sun rises above the trees before probing deep structure. They'll fish the shallow flats for aggressive fish, and when that bite slows, move to the deep weed edges and dropoffs. He, on the other hand, heads straight to the deep structure first thing in the morning.

LURES AND TECHNIQUES

Converse prefers lures that impact the bottom or the cover. Crankbaits and spinnerbaits are top choices.

"I want a lure that will deflect off the bottom or the cover to trigger impulse strikes," he describes. "A normal retrieve will get you bites from aggressive fish, but you can make a moody bass strike by causing the bait to dart erratically away from something."

If the water is less than 15 feet, he'll use a crankbait to bang and crash wildly along the outer edge of the cover. If the bait contacts the weeds, he hesitates the retrieve to allow it to back away, then rips the rod to pop it free.

His favorite for fishing grass, however, is a heavy Hildebrandt willowleaf spinnerbait that he slow rolls through the weeds.

The Carolina rig is one his favorites for testing unknown areas, especially away from heavy vegetation.

"The Carolina rig helps me determine the type of bottom, and that's really critical when looking for those deep honey holes," he explains. "I can feel that big sinker sliding through moss or banging on rocks and gravel. Big bass will really load up on those kinds of bottom transitions, and when I feel one, I know to slow down and work the area thoroughly."

When bass are relating tight to the weeds, Converse opts for a plastic worm. If the weather is stable, and he suspects the fish will be aggressive, he uses a 9- or 11-inch worm rigged Texas style.

However, if conditions are tough and the bite slow, he'll switch to a split shot style or Carolina rigged finesse worm and slow down. Jigs tipped with pork or large plastic trailers are another good choice, regardless of weather conditions.

Equipment also can make a big difference when fishing deep. Converse prefers rods at least 7 feet long because they're better for setting the hook in deep water.

"When using monofilament, you've got to move a lot of line to account for the stretch to set the hook on a long cast in deep water," he says. "Also, because lighter line tends to stretch more, I prefer 12- to 20-pound test in most situations. Sometimes I'll use no-stretch Berkley FireLine because it gives me a better feel and an instant hook set."

Weed Whacking

An experience with a Slug-Go and braided line in the lily pads gave Paul Converse an idea for fishing vegetation that has since become his favorite deep weed technique.

"Weed whacking" not only produces bass, but it also reduces the problem of weeds clogging in a spinnerbait and fouling the cast. It's deadly in deep weeds, where bass don't see many spinnerbaits.

"I was at Lake Guntersville, Ala., practicing for a tournament, and my spinnerbait kept fouling in weeds," Converse recalls. "Then I remembered the day I hooked a bass on the Slug-Go and how the braided line cut through the pads like a lawnmower."

Converse rigged his spinnerbait on a 7-foot fiberglass baitcast rod with 20-pound Berkley FireLine and began catching quality bass from the weeds. The almost indestructible, low stretch superline sliced through the cover, and the spinnerbait popped freely from the weeds.

"By keeping the rod tip pointed at the bait, I could pop the bait free by simply turning the reel handle faster," he describes. "If I tried to pull the bait free, the rod would sag and the bait still clogged. It's very important to hold the rod level and wind the lure directly toward the rod tip, turning the handle briskly when you feel it contact the weeds."

He prefers tin-headed, willowleaf Hildebrandt spinnerbaits in sizes from 1 to 1 1/4 ounces to help keep the bait down.

Converse casts the lure into the weeds then follows it down on a tight line. Some strikes occur as the bait falls, but most come after he's popped the bait free of weeds.

"It's just another way to trigger a reaction strike," he describes. "When a bass sees that bait jump out of the weeds and flutter, the fish nails it. There's never any doubt about the strike. You know it instantly."

The lure responds because of the lack of stretch in the FireLine, yet you need the limber fiberglass rod to absorb the shock of a big, hard pulling bass. Converse says you'll lose fewer fish because of it.

SHALLOW STRUCTURE

Unlock the secrets
to shallow water fishing
with this inside information . . .

BASS ON BARE BANKS

If an area looks like it ought to hold bass, maybe you'd do better fishing elsewhere

To THE PROFESSIONAL ANGLER, so-called "nothing water" is often what elevates them above the ever-improving ranks of tournament hopefuls.

The term, "nothing water," clearly holds a very tangible double meaning. These bland stretches of water only *look* unproductive. They don't have the cachet of visible cover, exposed rockpiles, obvious breaklines, docks or most of the other items that conjure up bass fishing daydreams. What they do hold are bass that have rarely been exposed to any degree of fishing pressure.

John Murray of Arizona, a perennial leader in western tournaments and others across the nation, knows well the value of finding offbeat water in the heavily trafficked and sparsely covered impoundments of the West.

"A renowned western bass fisherman, the late Art Price, would ask all the people at the marinas where fishermen never caught fish," recalls Murray. "Then he would go catch them in those areas. This same method can work for anyone. Just go to where you have never caught fish or where you have never heard of bass being caught."

World champion Jay Yelas concurs with this line of thinking. But he warns prospective "bare banks" fishermen that this technique, like everything else in bass fishing, is only learned through hard work.

To Yelas, the key is being able to recognize what the normal pattern should be based on seasonal influences, water temperature, weather patterns and the like. If you have trouble identifying the prevailing pattern, notes Yelas, this method of finding nothing water is not for you.

"You almost have to second-guess yourself," counsels Yelas. "The first thing is to figure out where the fish *should be* and what lures you *should be* working. On the BASS circuit, everyone is thinking those same thoughts, so the normal stuff often doesn't work. You have to go one step beyond."

What Murray and Yelas have discovered is often what prevents local anglers from rising above the professionals when the competition is held on their home water. Without being mentally restrained by what *should be*, the pros frequently

A CRANKBAIT is a productive locator bait for making contact with subtle bottom irregularities, which are key areas for catching bare bank bass.

discover productive water that local bass fishermen have routinely ignored.

Far from being a phenomenon of the West, where cover is at a premium and fishing pressure is intense, this ability to find overlooked water is equally critical in other parts of the bass fishing world.

"If you are not accustomed to what to look for, it can be difficult," admits Murray. "But every part of the country has keys to their nothing fishing. Whether it is rock, bottom composition, grass, whatever — with some concerted effort you can pick it up in your area."

Of course, a key to nothing water is a lack of visible, productive-looking cover. Perhaps the best way to evaluate a potential area is this: If you look at a stretch of water and your heart starts to flutter with anticipation, chances are every other bass fisherman who sees it will feel the same way. Look elsewhere.

According to Yelas and Don Iovino, yet another western angler with solid roots in finesse, a good place to start looking is offshore.

"In spring, you don't have to be a rocket scientist to know where to fish," remarks Iovino. "But after the spring 'glory days,' those fish start moving out and getting on structure. That's when you have to learn to use your electronics and fish for that type of fish. I'm not talking just about deep water. I'm talking about banks and flats on the first or second breakline. It could be 10 feet of water or 8. It's just getting away from everything

IF YOU LOCATE a diamond in the rough, or an inconspicuous spot that attracts fish, you will likely have the place all to yourself.

that looks good and fishing what looks good *under* the water."

"If you've only got an hour, then just fish the bank," adds Yelas. "But, if you want an area that will produce a school of fish — a number of bass — you need to spend some time looking off-shore, whether it's a hump, extended point or ledge."

One of Iovino's tricks in dissecting an unfamiliar lake is to start out near the dam. His philosophy is that dam areas invariably hold fish and can provide you with a decent launching pad from which to find good nothing water. This search begins at the first, or primary, breakline, where the topography makes a significant drop. Whether the bottom drops 2 feet or 12, or whether the first break is at 5 feet deep or 10, you simply have to find this zone. It can vary dramatically from lake to lake.

In Iovino's vocabulary, a "break" is something with structure or cover on the drop; a "drop" is merely a change in bottom contour. To produce fish, he says, there must be something on the break.

Aside from finding a genuine "breakline," per-

THE EMPHASIS is not on finding shad on the electronics, but in locating areas with significant depth changes, proper bottom composition, and fish-holding structure.

haps the next element in importance is a hard bottom.

Bass generally do not frequent muddy zones and, even if baitfish aren't apparent, it's likely that they will be somewhere near breaks with hard bottoms.

Again, the emphasis is not on finding gamefish or bait on your electronics, but in locating areas with significant depth changes, proper bottom composition (denoted by a thick bottom line on sonar) and fish-holding structure. It is equally important to dial down your personal requirements as to what looks good. Remember, you're not looking for a Beverly Hills mansion in a luxuriant parklike setting. This is affordable bass housing.

Another methodology in finding nothing water is to look for something that most bass fishermen do everything to avoid: people. Swim beaches, boat ramps and jet-ski areas are just some of the "people places" John Murray rates as having excellent potential.

"I like to see shore anglers fishing for either crappie or bluegill," says Murray, "and I like skiers and swimmers along a bank. I like to see people who are not bass fishermen. Crappie fishermen, for example, are not after bass, but they usually keep the bass fishermen away."

Unlike many bass anglers, Murray isn't put off by skiers. He contends that bass in well-traveled areas become accustomed to the activity and actually feed more after the recreational boaters start churning up the water.

"Some nothing banks aren't productive early in the morning," he says. "But after jet-skiers start buzzing around and people begin swimming, the fish really start feeding. I think the bass are accustomed to that commotion spooking their food, making it easier for them to feed effectively."

As Yelas indicates, this is just another situation where an angler has to second-guess himself. Too often, bass fishermen limit themselves to the textbook notion of a calm, idyllic spot as being the only kind that can hold bass. But bass can't

read. Instead, they must often carve out a niche despite the furor above the surface.

While it takes some time to mentally readjust your thinking into a nothing-water format, the effort can pay off handsomely. The pros know it.

NOTHING BAITS FOR NOTHING BANKS

In choosing lures for nothing water, the most daunting task is finding something that can seek out and draw strikes from bass holding in areas of sparse cover. The one-two-three combination mentioned most often by the pros involves crankbaits, Carolina rigs and split shot gear.

Far from being a desperation ploy, a crankbait is often very effective in nothing water, because these relatively untouched bass can be very aggressive. They haven't seen a torrent of cranks, reminds Murray, and frequently respond with what appears to be uncharacteristic aggression. If he can get the fish to go on a crankbait, Murray sticks to it. He does prefer, however, to use a Carolina rig or split shot bait to locate fish.

The key to crankbait productivity in nothing water is accurately gauging the feeding intensity of the day. On some days, the crankbait will only turn up the most aggressive fish. On other days, it may well be the bait of choice. For the fisherman just beginning to learn the ways of nothing areas, the Carolina rig or split shot approach will probably be the best bet for catching these fish, counsels Yelas.

A SINGLE PIECE of cover can be the only element holding fish on a bare bank, meaning these areas will replenish themselves and can be fished frequently throughout the day.

While they may look similar, Carolina rigging and split shotting are two decidedly different tactics. More suited to heavier weights — from 1/2 to 1 ounce — and larger plastics, such as lizards, the Carolina rig is usually drift-fished or worked in a slower, more traditional lift-and-move retrieve. Baitcasting gear is *de rigeur* with Carolina rigs, as are longer rods in the 6- to 7-foot category.

On the other hand, split shotting is generally a steadier, faster moving retrieve, using smaller, 4-inch curled-tail worms or grubs and lighter lines in the 6- to 8-pound range. The lighter line demands spinning gear with shorter rods in 5 1/2- to 6-foot lengths.

With these three methods, you can pretty much stair-step down in subtlety from crankbaits to Carolina rigs to split shot, as fishing conditions dictate. In their own way, each is an excellent coverage technique as well as being a productive method to capitalize on those key isolated areas normally associated with nothing water.

Recognizing the importance of these techniques is as crucial to your success as learning how to fish each effectively. If you attempt to fish nothing water with only one method, you will be disappointed with your long-term results. Occasionally, crankbaits, Carolina rigs or split shot baits alone will mop up on bass in these offbeat areas. Most often, it will be a combination of things, since even bass in nothing water have various feeding moods.

HOW TO FISH ROCKY BANKS AND BLUFFS

Steep, sheer banks are virtually untapped hideouts for bass through most of the year

Y ou can take that to the bank" is a phrase that means virtually the same thing in the world of finance and bass fishing. The subject in question is a cinch, a sure bet, a producer.

The only difference is, the moneymen deposit into banks, while anglers withdraw from them — specifically from deep, rocky banks and bluffs.

Two such "investors" are veteran BASS pro Basil Bacon of Missouri and renowned lure maker and pro angler Gary Yamamoto of Texas. These anglers are steep-bank specialists. The former fishes Ozark style, with lunker-size baits and stout tackle. Yamamoto, a former Arizonian, specializes in Western "finesse" tactics. But regardless of their differences in geography and preferred fishing methods, Bacon and Yamamoto agree in one major area. . . .

"When it comes to deep banks and bluffs, you're talking about places that can be fished year-round. Now, sometimes you may have more bass in other areas of the lake, but you can just about always count on finding some fish on a bluff. This is a good, dependable spot," says Bacon.

"Steep rocky banks and bluffs provide everything bass need: food, cover, shade and deep water. So it's easy to understand why they stay around this structure. All a fisherman needs to learn are a few basic locations and presentations, and he can catch fish off deep banks and bluffs in any season," Yamamoto confides.

(Opposite Page) POINTS, ROCKSLIDES, cracks and other irregular features are key bass hideouts along rocky bluffs.

THE FOUR SEASON APPROACH

Bacon learned to fish on Lake of the Ozarks and Table Rock Lake in Missouri, and Bull Shoals Lake, which spans the Missouri/Arkansas border. These are typical highland reservoirs that run clear and deep, with channels that snake through Ozark ridges. Quite commonly, these channels are bordered by limestone bluffs that run for a half mile or more.

These bluffs typically include small pockets, coves and slide-ins that break the

BECAUSE IT can be worked vertically down the sides of structure, a tube jig is a highly effective lure for bluff banks.

DEPENDING ON THE season, smallmouth will move vertically through the water column of a bluff bank.

secondary structure break, like a deep ledge with timber on it, or a stretch with several small rock shelves or irregularities. To find the bass, Bacon works his way along the bluff, trying such spots. "I don't fish all the bluff. I'll try one area, then move a little and try another area," he explains.

In the process, he uses four main lures: a 1/2- or 5/8-ounce rubber skirted jig (brown or black) dressed with a No. 1 pork frog; a nickel or bronze jigging spoon; a twinspin spinnerbait; and a deep running crankbait. He alternates these baits, matching them to the type of spot he's fishing.

"Usually I'll hop a jig-and-pig down the bluff face, or I'll jig a spoon or a twinspin vertically over a deep ledge," he says. "Or I might move my boat in next to the structure and make long casts with a crankbait parallel to the bluff."

Besides experimenting to find the right location, Bacon also tests different depths.

"In winter, bluff bass are as unpredictable as the weather. One day can be warm and pretty, and I'll catch fish 35 to 40 feet deep. Then the next day it's snowing, the wind's blowing and it's miserable, and the fish will be up in 2 feet of water. So I just start from the top and go to the bottom."

When Bacon exhausts all his options without finding fish, he goes back and works the most promising areas of the bluff with light spinning gear and either a plastic-skirted jig or a 1/8- or 1/4-ounce jig and pork strip. "Sometimes they'll bite the little slow baits when they won't hit the bigger, faster moving ones," he notes.

When he does locate bluff bass in the winter, "there's usually a school of them, and they won't move much from one day to the next. They may move 100 yards or so or change their depth, but they'll stick pretty close to the same general location."

continuity of the rock wall and add variety to the structure. Bluffs may also contain any combination of lateral shelves, secondary ledges, submerged timber and other features.

Bacon says bass are drawn to these breaks in the structure, and they are where he concentrates his fishing efforts. He adds that the fish hold in different zones along bluffs at different times of the year. So the key to bluff fishing success is matching the right zones and times, then using baits and techniques that are compatible with the particular structure and season.

BLUFFS IN MIDWINTER

Bacon says that in winter, the bass hold along the face of the bluff, and oftentimes they will relate to a

BLUFFS IN PRESPAWN AND SPAWN PERIODS

The prespawn and spawning periods are prime times for catching bass off bluffs. Basil Bacon says rising water temperature triggers the fish to move to predictable locations, and their appetites grow healthy.

"When the water temperature climbs into the mid-40s, the bass move into small, shallow gravel pockets along the bluff's face, especially south-facing pockets that catch direct sunlight," he says. "These places warm up first, and the fish come into them to feed." Bacon works these spots with a jig-and-pig or slow swimming crankbait.

As water temperature continues to rise, the bass migrate to the ends of the bluff, to the primary points where the channel swings in or where coves jut back in from the bluff. Bacon sometimes finds these fish in the first good-size pockets off the ends of the bluff.

Now the bass are increasingly active, and Bacon relies more and more on crankbaits.

"I'll try an assortment of baits," he says. "Sometimes the fish will be up in 2 to 4 feet of water, and they might want a tiny crankbait or a shallow diving jerkbait like a Long A Bomber or a Rebel or Rogue. Or if they're deeper, I'll cast the points with a long, deep diving minnow, like the Spoonbill Rebel. I'll add lead to the bait so it'll just barely float. Then I'll crank it down close to the bottom and fish it with slow, sweeping pulls with my rod tip."

When the water temperature climbs into the 60s, the fish get serious about spawning, and Bacon alters his bluff fishing tactics again. "If a lake has a lot of good, shallow spawning areas, most bass will leave the bluffs and deep banks to make

AFTER THE SPAWN, many bass that were in the coves migrate back to main channel areas. They will rejoin fish that nested along the bluffs, where they will feed wherever they can trap baitfish.

Gary Yamamoto:
Fishing Bluffs In Western Lakes

Lure innovator Gary Yamamoto once lived on Lake Powell, which is gin clear and lined with rocks. Bluffs and deep banks are the primary structures, and anglers on this and other Western impoundments learn to fish the "minerals" out of necessity. Yamamoto has learned that bass react the same anywhere, and techniques he uses for fishing bluffs and deep banks in the West will slay Eastern bass under similar conditions.

Yamamoto emphasizes that under the clear water and intense sunlight conditions in the Southwest, bass hang back in the shadows, where rocks block the sun's rays. So, in effect, the shadows position the fish, and this is a crucial part of this angler's bluff/deep bank pattern.

"Look for the fish where there is broken structure, say, rough banks as opposed to smooth ones," advises the Texas pro. "These could be jagged rocks or rock slides, any bank with wrinkles instead of an even surface. These places are where your shadows will be, and they're also where the fish will stay."

What is more, Yamamoto likes what he calls "transition areas, or those seams where rough banks meet smooth ones, or where sloping shorelines become more vertical.

"You find these places with your eyes, not a map or depthfinder," Yamamoto coaches. "You just run the lake and watch for any place that fits this description. Usually, what you see above the water surface continues on beneath it, so if you find transition structure on the bank, it'll extend down into the lake."

their nests, but a few big fish will still spawn along the bluffs, usually a little later than the ones back in the shallows. I always try for these fish. I'll stick with the same points and little pockets, but now I'll switch to topwater baits, like a Zara Spook or a Rapala, and I'll also throw spinnerbaits. I'll fish close to the bank, a lot of times casting parallel along the bluff. If I don't find them right next to the rocks, I'll throw out in a little deeper water."

TOP SPOTS FOR FINDING BASS ALONG BLUFFS/ROCK BANKS Key locations for bass along steep banks include bluff points, small pockets and indentations, points along bluff faces, rock slides and ledges along bluffs.

Small pocket or indentation in bluff face

Main bluff point (especially good in prespawn)

Points of small coves jutting back from bluff

Rock slides and/or unusually rough rock formations

Ledges where channel cuts away from bluff

BLUFFS IN LATE SPRING AND SUMMER

After the spawn, many bass that were in the coves migrate back to main channel areas, and they rejoin fish that nested along the bluffs. Now these fish begin roaming the bluff faces, feeding wherever they can trap baitfish.

"This time of year, most feeding activity will be shallower than it was in winter," he says. "This is a prime time to try one particular type of place that can provide some of the best fishing you'll ever find along bluffs," Bacon notes. "If you can catch a lake level down several feet, you can go check a bluff and mark places where little cracks or crevices run horizontally along the bluff's face. Usually these aren't too impressive-looking. They are just 1 or 2 feet high and 2 or 3 feet back in the bluff. Also, most of these cracks have little ledges sticking out on the bottom side. In summer, when the water covers them back up, bass love to hide back in these places." Bacon adds that bright sunshine is a strict requirement for this pattern to pay off.

"You catch them by holding the boat right against the bluff. Then you flip a heavy jig ahead of the boat right next to the rocks. If you can hit that ledge and bounce the jig up and down a few times right in front of a bunch of big fish's noses, one of them is going to get it. This is when you'd better have strong line on your reel, because the bass is going back under those rocks, and it will cut the line."

Bacon says one other specialty presentation effective in summer is retrieving walking baits along bluff faces and across points in the middle of the day.

BLUFFS WITH THE ADDED BONUS
of standing timber will move the
fish out farther from a bluff than
similar areas void of trees.

Tackle And Techniques for Bluffs

Because Gary Yamamoto doesn't have to make a lot of casts on any given bluff structure, he can afford to be slower and more precise with his presentation. Accordingly, he mainly fishes plastic grubs and worms to lure bass out of the rocks.

"My standard is a 1/4-ounce jighead and a 5-inch grub," he says. "I'll fish this on 8-pound-test line with a special 7-foot baitcasting rod that I designed and sell through my tackle company."

Yamamoto says the long rod provides extra leverage for setting the hook on deep bass.

In the lure department, he alternates between a standard single- or double-tail swimming grub and his Hula grub, which features a molded-in skirt.

"If the bass are aggressive, I use the Hula grub," he says. "It has more action to tantalize the fish. But if they're not very active, I'll use the plainer, more subtle grub.

"It's important to bounce it off the structure, to keep the bait tight to the cover," he says. "So I hold my boat out and cast in perpendicular to the bank, and then I let the bait sink. If I'm fishing a sheer wall that falls down to a 10-foot ledge, I'll throw right to that wall and then try to bounce it off the wall as it drops."

With this technique, he frequently allows his bait to fall on a slack line so it will drop straight down. "I watch my line and try to see strikes that I don't feel," he explains. "But a lot of times I take up the slack, and a fish is just suddenly there. It has the bait."

The bottom line on fishing bluffs and steep banks is that these are always options for catching bass. In certain lakes and under the right conditions, this structure may be the best option. In other lakes and circumstances, more bass may be located elsewhere. But the fact remains that if a lake has bluffs and deep banks, these spots will almost always attract some segment of the bass population, and anglers should know how to fish them. Then if shallow water bass quit biting, bluffs and deep banks are a prime backup pattern.

BLUFF BASS IN FALL

"In early fall, a lot of fish migrate back up the creeks, and they don't return to the main lake until the water temperature drops into the low 50s," Bacon continues. "So, this means late fall is the best time of this season to fish bluffs and deep banks. But when that temperature hits this range, bluffs can be a predominant place to fish."

In this period, Bacon casts to the same places he did in the spring: main and secondary bluff points, small pockets along the bluff face, slide-ins and other structure breaks. He relies mostly on spinnerbaits and, to a lesser degree, topwaters. Then, as the water temperature continues falling, he reverts back to a jig-and-pig and fishes deeper as the bass slide down the structure and into their winter patterns.

"This is an excellent time to catch big fish along bluffs," Bacon notes. "If I'm in a fall tournament, and I catch a limit back in the coves, a lot of times I'll move out to the main channel and fish bluffs to try to improve my weight."

BEATING THE BANK BEATERS

Here's what to do when your favorite bass banks are crowded with other anglers

You begin the day filled with confidence as you head to a productive stretch of bank where you caught bass the week before.

But your hopes sink as you arrive to find another angler working "your" spot. You move on to your backup bank, only to find a couple of other boats have beaten you to it. Frustration mounts as

you try to decide what to do.

You consider leapfrogging around them to reach the front of the line, but you know that would be rude. Instead, you quietly slip to the rear of the line of boats parading down the bank and prepare yourself for a slow day.

At various times of year, the bass bite dictates that

anglers crowd the same shallow water. Everyone but those with the fastest boats spend the day fishing "used water."

Similarly, tournament anglers are often crowded into those areas of the lake that have historically produced the biggest bags of fish. Two very successful tournament anglers — former Bassmaster Classic Champion Ken Cook and BASS record setter Robert Lee — have faced similar conditions throughout their professional careers. Cook and Lee have learned to adjust both their approach and presentation to beat other "bank beaters."

THE AGE-OLD QUESTION

Indeed, there are those times — such as during large tournaments or on weekends — when fishermen can expect plenty of pressure on the areas they plan to fish. When pulling up to a crowded area, Cook says, an angler must first determine whether to move on or stay put.

"Do you want to fish an area where you know there's a lot of fish and lots of competition for those fish, or do you want to move to an area with fewer fish and very little competition?" suggests Cook. "That's an age-old question."

When deciding to stay and compete, the best tactic is often to try to show the fish something different. "To do so," explains Cook, "we must know what the other anglers are fishing. If most are throwing a 6-inch Texas rigged worm, I'll downsize to a tube bait or small craw worm. I will fish a bait that's appropriate for the situation, but one that's different from what the guys ahead of me are using."

Often, other boats are close enough to see the specific bait the anglers are fishing. However, there are times when it isn't possible to see exactly what the competition is throwing. When unable to see the lure, Cook watches the anglers' casting techniques — whether it be an overhead cast, flipping or pitching, or a sidearm cast.

Cook also looks for boat positioning and the speed at which the boat is moving down the bank. "You might not be able to see *what* they're fishing," he adds, "but you can often see *how* they're fishing. You can tell whether they're fishing slowly and deliberately, or are quickly covering water. If the guy ahead of me is fishing like Guido Hibdon — making 100 casts to the same laydown — I am going to fish something totally different, like a reaction bait."

Like Cook, California's Robert Lee often looks for the reaction bite when following other boats down a bank. Unlike many other western anglers, Lee rarely downsizes his baits when countering angling pressure. Instead, he constantly changes his presentations. For example, after ripping a spinnerbait by a target to get the bass excited, he will often follow that with a slower retrieve to draw the reaction strike.

DIFFERENT STROKES

Robert Lee's success in winning four consecutive BASS events on the Sacramento/San Joaquin River Delta occurred when the fishery was swarming with both tournament and leisure anglers. Still, Lee was able to outfish the crowd to victory each time. The key was his ability to make precise, calculated presentations.

"On the Delta, you really have to consider how the bass are positioned in the current," explains Lee. "You have to figure out what type of cover the bass are using and how they relate to it, and you need to know what the fish are willing to hit. That changes from hour to hour."

CONSIDER MODIFYING spinnerbaits in highly pressured situations. Downsizing or using a different type of blade can make all the difference.

These factors — cover and orientation — are just as important on other western fisheries, says Lee, especially when bass are shallow.

"Out West, a lot of us beat the banks," says Lee. "In fact, it's my favorite way to fish. But it can be one of the toughest ways to win a tournament simply because angling pressure can be so high in shallow water."

Lee overcomes the competition with precise lure placement. Using such information as current direction, wind, shade and others, he determines exactly where in a piece of cover the bass should be holding. Then he places his lures softly and naturally in those spots.

Most bank beaters are running down the bank, he says, chucking and winding without considering how bass are oriented to cover or how they should best be approached. Instead, they haphazardly cover water and, consequently, experience little success.

"When fishing that shallow water," explains Lee, "you have to be more attentive as to how you approach the fish. In clear water, targeting shallow bass is more like hunting — you almost have to sneak up on them and make long, accurate and quiet casts."

GO YOUR OWN WAY

A second option when faced with crowded conditions is to abandon the more popular areas and find spots that receive less pressure. Ken Cook knows from his own tournament experience that this strategy can pay big dividends.

Many years ago, while fishing a pro championship event on Texas' Lake Granbury, Cook decided to let other anglers fight for the obvious hot spots while he concentrated on out-of-the-way areas.

Most everyone targeted points extending to creek channels. The structures were obvious and, predictably, they attracted a number of anglers. However, the featureless flats found on the backside of the same channel swings were completely ignored.

"I decided to get as far away as I could from the more popular channel bends," Cook relates. "I knew there would be fewer fish in the unpopular areas, but I knew those few fish would be all mine."

Cook was able to spend the entire competition day fishing the flat by himself. Although bass weren't plentiful there, they were more cooperative than those being harassed by other anglers, and they were very accessible.

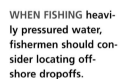

WHEN FISHING heavily pressured water, fishermen should consider locating offshore dropoffs.

"Often, I prefer to target a different group of fish than the rest of the crowd simply because I like having the fish all to myself," notes Cook. "The area may only give up 10 bites, but because I am the only boat in there, all 10 bites are potentially mine. Conversely, a more popular area may give up 60 bites, but because there will be 20 boats fishing it, they're only getting three fish per boat." Cook likes his odds better.

BACKING OFF THE OBVIOUS

Another way to find an ignored, underfished group of bass in the more popular areas is to simply back off the bank a bit.

For example, if most other anglers are focusing on areas where creek channels sweep up against a bank, you can look for similar channel bends in open water, away from shore. To fish the less obvious features effectively, you'll have to employ a depthfinder and marker buoys. Because these areas are tougher to locate, the bass they hold should receive less angling pressure.

"That same scenario is often true with breaks in shallow water," explains Cook. "The change in water color typically marks the first break in water depth, so it gets fished hard. However, if you'll move farther out, you might find a second, less visible drop that will hold more bass. That second break typically goes unfished."

SUNBAKED BANKS

Among Lee's favorite "ugly banks" in early spring and late fall are featureless banks baked by the sun. These areas offer warmer water than the shady banks other anglers are prowling, and Lee often finds them swarming with baitfish.

"A lot of anglers overlook these banks during this time of year," Lee reports. "They go to a rocky bank with lots of boulders and cover and, of course, lots of shade. They will zip past the sunbaked, barren banks on their way to other areas."

THE CHOICE IS YOURS

In essence, when the banks are being pounded by other anglers, you have two choices. You can follow the crowds but employ different lures and presentations, or you can look for less productive — and less pressured — water.

"When faced with heavy angling pressure, you have to make a decision," says Cook. "And in a tournament, this decision will break or make you."

ROBERT LEE'S favorite early season banks are those baked by the afternoon sun. Fish will be attracted to these banks first.

Finding Beauty In Ugly Banks

When angling pressure is heavy, Robert Lee often targets "ugly banks" — ones that appear so featureless and void of fish that most fishermen fly right by without giving the water a second thought.

"I have never seen an ugly bank that didn't have something below the water surface that held fish," says Lee. "That unseen feature might be a cut or a slight ridge, stumps or brush. I have done surprisingly well — including winning tournaments — by fishing ugly banks like that."

Lee will often pull up to a featureless bank, pull out his topo map of the lake and search for an ever so slight hiccup in the contour line. Any little deviation in a relatively smooth contour can be the key to finding a half-dozen good fish, he says. Scanning the breakline with his depthfinder often turns up a small rock slide or stumpbed capable of holding a small group of fish.

"You're not going to catch a dozen fish from this type of area," Lee acknowledges. "But you might catch two or three good ones there. Because these areas mostly go unmolested, the fish you find there usually are bigger ones."

FISHING THE FLATS

Few anglers fish flats as thoroughly as they should. Here's what they're missing

LESS IS MORE. Whether it is architecture, art or even life itself, this philosophy celebrates the inherent joys of simplicity. Of course, this implies that we must first be able to recognize and understand these elegant basics before we can truly appreciate them.

For humans, this is usually where we get into trouble. Instead of finding contentment in *less*, we rush headlong after *more*. In bass fishing, this is a common affliction.

Perhaps nowhere is it expressed more clearly than in fishing the flats, those relatively shallow, often expansive areas where cover may mean a scattered handful of submerged bushes or a breakline that barely registers a sonar blip.

Without question, it is not the stuff of which bass fishing dreams are made. In fact, the very things that make them so productive are often the things that deter most fishermen.

"The perfect flat has cover so sparse that most people won't stop there to fish it," notes veteran pro angler Rob Kilby of Hot Springs, Ark. "Most people figure that it's just too much hassle to fish one little spot and then go to all the trouble of cranking up and moving somewhere else."

The very same mind-set holds true regardless of the compass point.

For veteran Tennessee pro Charlie Ingram, the resistance to flats is a confusing one, since the bass found in these areas are active, feeding fish and generally easier to catch. The same holds true out West, where anglers who should be more comfortable working barren terrain also avoid flats in favor of more textbook bass fishing environments, says western native Dean Rojas, one of bass fishing's most versatile anglers.

DEFINING A FLAT

The size and depth of flats vary widely from region to region and from lake to lake. However, a typical flat will slope very gradually from the shoreline out (sometimes hundreds of yards) to a breakline (depth change) where it meets the main lake or a creek channel. Depending on the lake, this outside break can be very subtle (measured in increments of 1 or 2 feet) or extremely steep and abrupt (such as those found in the Colorado River lakes).

From the shoreline to the outermost breakline,

A CAROLINA RIG is the hands-down favorite for covering large flats. It is also an effective bait for locating and making contact with isolated cover.

there can be multiple breaks in between. While these intermediate breaklines can be very subtle, they nonetheless represent significant depth changes that can be used by bass moving across the flat.

While just about any flat of any depth will hold fish, the most common scenario is a flat that eventually slopes down to 10 or 15 feet at the outer breakline. However, it should be noted that the different water depths on flats will be more productive at different times of the year, making seasonal considerations an important element in flats fishing strategy.

PICKING A FLAT

To the untrained eye, flats appear remarkably similar. But, there are several important keys that

can eliminate some flats and put others on the "must fish" list.

• *Contours* — Chief among these attributes is the presence of a creek, ditch, culvert or cut that runs across the flat.

"One of the most important things I look for is flats with ditches. But there doesn't need to be anything more than a 6-inch variation in depth," observes Ingram. "I may not catch the fish in that ditch, but it gives them a pathway onto and off the flat."

If the creek or depth contour is not significant enough to be shown on a topographic map, many times it can be observed simply by looking for contour changes along the shoreline.

• *Cover* — Even if a flat offers no discernible

CONTOURS, structure and water clarity are three criteria for evaluating the productivity of a flat.

ditch or cut, isolated cover can make the most imposing flat into a worthwhile opportunity. For Kilby, the scarcity of cover is not viewed as a negative factor, but one that merely shrinks a huge flat down to manageable size.

"The key to flats fishing is isolated cover — two or three pieces of cover (stumps, brush, rocks or even floating logs stuck in the mud) scattered across a large area. All of these will hold a fish, and will be replenished within an hour after catching a bass from them."

The problem with flats that offer an abundance of cover, notes Kilby, is their attractiveness to other anglers. These easy-to-identify holding areas get pounded regularly, while less obvious flats (with sparse, submerged cover) go unmolested.

• *Water Clarity* — Although water clarity can be a hindrance in that it can make already fidgety flats bass even more wary, it can be a tremendous aid in finding isolated cover. At times, finding the right flat demands scanning the area for signs of prime, isolated cover or bottom irregularities.

If the water is stained, a spinnerbait or crankbait can be used to "feel your way" through the flat to uncover key areas, counsels Rojas. "I try to find stuff that isn't getting pounded. I first look

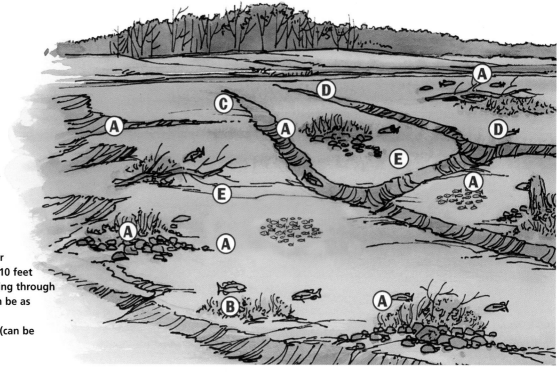

FLATS HOT SPOTS
A) Sparse, isolated cover
B) Outside breakline at 10 feet
C) Ditch or culvert running through flat (depth variation can be as slight as 6 inches).
D) Secondary breakline (can be very subtle).
E) Baitfish

Flats Keys

The primary emphases in developing a flats strategy include:

■ Wind influences lure selection. Calm conditions allow for topwater presentations. Windy weather shifts the focus to spinnerbaits or crankbaits. Really forceful breezes can push fishermen right off the flats.

■ Don't be deterred by flats with sparse, isolated cover.

■ Fit your presentations and lures to the conditions and seasons.

■ Move quickly to learn what a flat has to offer, and file these observations for future reference.

■ Keep in mind that while flats bass are aggressive, they are also very spooky. The clearer the water, the longer the casts and faster the retrieves required.

■ Key on irregularities in the flat, whether this means isolated cover, ditches or breaklines.

■ Let the fish guide your decisions on staying or leaving an area. Don't beat a dead horse.

for key elements like ditches, rocks or points, and I follow those in and start looking for isolated cover or brush.

"If you catch them there, great. But if you don't, then you should work the flat, 'nothing' areas. At lakes Mead or Havasu, some anglers don't key on these places; they go right to the cuts or points of the flats without working the inside areas. So many times, I've caught a few in the cuts and then moved 50 yards to get a 3- or 4-pounder on a nothing-looking flat."

PICKING APART A FLAT

Ingram, Kilby and Rojas differ somewhat regarding which season is most productive for flats fishing. But that merely confirms how different fishing styles and regional variations make flats fairly consistent regardless of the season.

• *Spring* — In the spring, one key to a productive flat is the presence of deeper water nearby — coupled with a northeast position on the lake that receives the most direct sunlight and therefore warms faster. Generally, flats with a harder bottom composition (gravel, hard clay or rocky substrate) will attract more spawning fish.

As fish begin staging on the deeper breakline during prespawn, one of Kilby's best patterns is working a jerkbait along the edge of the break to intercept suspended bass. This method is particularly efficient if the wind is blowing. If not, a Carolina rig pulled off the edge can be just as effective.

This outside edge is also a prime prespawn area for Rojas, who uses jigs and larger 6- to 8-inch worms on split shot rigs for big females waiting their turn to spawn.

As the season shifts into the spawn, a variety of baits — from spinnerbaits to floating worms — can be very effective for bass spread out across the flats. The only glitch now is that bass may be located at various depths throughout the flat, making certain patterns less dependable.

• *Postspawn/Summer* — With postspawn conditions, the fish begin migrating off the flat and hold along the deeper edge. Generally, any isolated cover or structure irregularity along that edge will yield fish.

GENERALLY, any isolated cover or structure irregularity along the edge of a flat will hold fish. Flipping and pitching are very effective in this situation.

Rojas believes that although many bass move deeper during this period, some groups of fish remain shallow.

"You won't find the numbers," cautions Rojas, "but when you find one, it's usually one worth catching."

With overcast or low light conditions, summer bass can be found shallow in 6 inches of water or out on the break in 10 to 15 feet as the sun rises.

But as the summer progresses, bass tend to lock in to prime holding areas. Unless the water is off-colored, an angler can pretty much eliminate the extreme shallows.

• *Fall* — The dependability of flat patterns on a day-to-day basis (not week-to-week) perhaps is best expressed in the fall. However, the link between baitfish and bass during this period is precisely what makes this a favorite flats time for Ingram.

During the fall, wind becomes an integral component of a flats strategy as the food chain moves with the wind-driven currents. To work a flat more effectively (and avoid spooking fish in the process), Ingram tries to stay off the trolling motor and use the wind to move his boat. He sometimes employs a drift sock to slow his progress.

For Kilby, wind — or the lack of it — dictates the area or areas of a flat where he will focus his attention.

"A 100-acre flat may have 100 bass on it," he suggests. "When the wind blows for maybe three or four consecutive days, it moves most of the bait to one corner of that flat, and probably 95 percent of the bass will be in that spot. When the wind switches around and the bait disperses, so will the bass. In a nutshell, wind isolates fish in one area of a flat and no wind isolates fish on cover."

• *Winter* — Clearly a tougher proposition in most cases, flats fishing can be productive late in the winter season and very early in the spring for anglers plying deeper flats that drop off in 12 to 15 feet of water.

FLATS TACTICS

While the methods used in attacking a flat can vary, the standard format when bass are active and aggressive involves a relatively fast pace with lures that cover large amounts of water effectively. In most cases, this means a spinnerbait, buzzbait or crankbait.

However, to move quickly across a flat and do so without spooking fish, an angler needs to keep the trolling motor speed constant and steady. Obviously, the more familiar a fisherman is with a particular flat, the faster he or she can move without running up unexpectedly on isolated targets.

Clear water makes the situation even more difficult, since the bass will naturally be more sensitive to fishing pressure. To combat this, longer casts and faster retrieves are required. In particular, bass seem to be more speed conscious in summer and fall.

One advantage of clear water comes when several fish follow a hooked bass to the boat. For veteran clear water fishermen like Rojas, these fish can eventually be caught, and they deserve further attention. On the other hand, if a flat is only turning up a fish here or there, it generally deserves just one pass. Where baitfish are abundant, a number of passes might be warranted.

Conversely, as water clarity diminishes in stained or muddy water, slower and more deliberate presentations are required. When using spinnerbaits, this generally demands switching from a willowleaf to a rounder blade (Colorado or Indiana) and slowing the retrieve.

Determining where to start on a flat is first dictated by the season, but can be influenced by one's personal experience. Although Rojas tends to start on the outside breakline in Western impoundments with clear water, Kilby generally goes to the bank and works his way out. In his experience, the outside sections receive the most attention from other anglers, and the fish there seem to be smaller.

"I've just been burned too many times doing it the other way," admits Kilby.

Spawning Grounds

When bass commence spawning, world champion BASS angler George Cochran sometimes finds them relating to stumps on flats in creeks. While the location is generally the same as in the fall, the pattern is decidedly different.

In spring, bass disperse throughout a stumpfield rather than concentrate on key locations near creek channels. Because a thick layer of silt coats the bottoms of most flats, the bass spawn on the only hard surfaces available — the tops of the stumps and their root systems.

Cochran took advantage of this pattern when he won a BASS tournament held on Lake Guntersville, Ala., with a three day catch of 55 pounds, 1 ounce. He found the bass in a bay off a major creek that contained a wide flat underneath water ranging from 2 to 4 feet deep. Scattered throughout the flat were roughly 200 stumps. Viewed through polarized sunglasses, most stumps appeared in the dingy water as dark spots beneath the surface.

"The only time I could see the bass," recalls the Arkansas legend, "was when I got too close and they'd spook away. I had to hold the boat well back from a stump and cast 4 or 5 feet past it. Then I'd swim the bait up and let it fall right on top of the stump."

On the first two days of the event, Cochran wielded a baitcasting rod with 10-pound line and duped the bass with a 1/4-ounce jig-and-pork combo.

RIVERS & STREAMS

Moving water is the place to be when current is a factor . . .

HOW THE PROS FISH BIG RIVERS

A seasonal guide to bass locations in major rivers

ALTHOUGH BASS FISHING traditionally takes place on large lakes and reservoirs, many major BASS events are routinely staged on major rivers, including such famous waterways as the Potomac, James, Columbia, Tennessee, Ohio, St. Lawrence and St. Johns.

Major rivers like these present an entirely different set of rules than those normally found on reservoirs, not the least of which may be the presence of current, tides, saltwater intrusion, barge traffic, reefs and shifting sandbars. In some instances, a particular river may actually have enough features to be fished like a lake, but not always.

"The best part about fishing big rivers is that most of them are not particularly clear; mud, silt, plankton and other factors provide some color to

STUDY A MAP to locate tributaries, backwaters and other features along a river where bass concentrate.

the water," explains former world champion Ken Cook. "That means bass live in shallow water. If there is a general rule that applies to river fishing, it is that you basically eliminate the deep water alternative.

"River bass also tend to be more object oriented than bass in lakes, so it's easier to predict where they will be located. They're not necessarily any easier to catch than lake bass, especially since everyone can concentrate on the same targets, but at least you usually have visible casting targets and a water depth that's comfortable."

"Very often, it's a shoreline fishery," adds Nevada pro Byron Velvick, who, like Cook, has fished rivers throughout the United States. "While that doesn't automatically mean the bass will be easier to catch, it usually does mean you can concentrate on a specific lure and presentation technique.

"On the downside," he continues, "slight changes in water conditions on a river can make major differences in where and how bass may be caught. I think the reason is that river conditions can change more rapidly than lake conditions, and river bass basically don't have as many habitat options as lake fish. When things go haywire in a river, the bass really shut down."

Velvick and Cook agree that the primary factor anglers must understand for successful river bass fishing is current, which plays an important role in bass behavior at different seasons of the year.

"Current is usually more important in summer and winter," explains Velvick, "Current also normally means cooler water in summer and more stable water temperatures in the winter."

When fishing current, Cook suggests anglers concentrate in places where the flow is obstructed by a jetty, boat dock, duck blind or even a large rock. All these objects create eddies that offer fish respite from the constant flow. In the calmer water behind these obstacles, bass lie in wait to feed on baitfish and other forage being washed past them. Essentially, bass want to be out of current but very near it.

"Current often allows fish to be more reactive," points out the former world champion, "which in turn can make them more predictable. If a bass is going to react to a morsel of food floating past, it has to react immediately, even when the water is colder.

"This is why fishing current is one of the best and most reliable patterns for winter fishing, especially if you can get into a headwater area such as right below a hydropower dam. Water temperatures are usually more stable in this type of current, so bass do not react as drastically to cold fronts and storms. The bite in winter may not be as dramatic, but it is usually reliable."

The time honored technique of casting upstream and letting current wash a lure beside cover and into eddy pockets is certainly one way to fish moving water, but it is by no means the only presentation. Because some large current breaks will hold numerous bass, continually casting just to one edge may attract only one or two fish; Cook recommends fishing big cover from as many angles as possible.

"We oftentimes see this on the Potomac," he notes. "One of the most famous fishing areas on the entire river is a graveyard of barges known as the Arkindale Flats, where bass are out of the current but near it. The best way to fish that spot is by moving in and out of the old barges and casting from a hundred different angles."

FISH A SPINNERBAIT in moving water because it emulates baitfish, which are moving targets to the bass.

Target-specific lures, like jigs and plastic worms, are among the best choices for current conditions, but crankbaits, spinnerbaits and even an occasional topwater can be used, depending on the size and configuration of the cover. Crankbaiters often do very well on the long, angular wing dams of the Arkansas and Red rivers, for instance, while jigs and worms usually rule the rock filled shallows of the upper Chattahoochee above Lake Eufaula.

One of Cook's favorite river current techniques is fishing the outside bends of a river, especially spots where brush has accumulated. In places like these, the cover might be completely under the surface, so the Oklahoma pro usually stays with weedless lures, like worms and grubs, at least until he has a "feel" for what he's actually probing.

Other places to look for current can be at the mouths of tributaries that flow into a river or in narrow cuts between larger areas of open water. In this latter situation, the current may be wind induced, but it can still produce tremendous action at times.

"You analyze current the way you study any other type of cover or structure," says Velvick. "On Pickwick Lake on the Tennessee River, you use different lures according to where you happen to be fishing. Just below the Wilson Dam, one of the fa-

vorite smallmouth techniques is jigging a spoon as you float downstream; the water is deep enough to do that.

"A few miles down the lake, however, the preferred technique is letting the current wash a 1/8-ounce grub on 6- and 8-pound-test line through shallow stumps. You just have to study the conditions you're facing and determine the most efficient way to present a lure."

Whenever he can, Velvick prefers fishing backwaters, those shallow, woody/weedy sloughs and pools completely off the main river. Traditionally, backwaters have little or no current and can be fished more like small lakes.

"For me, the key to any backwater is depth," he says. "Ideally, a backwater pool will have a different water color (slightly green, indicating plankton), a visible food supply (jumping minnows) and a good depth change (such as a channel or series of ditches).

"The overall size of a backwater area is not as important as depth, because in my experience, a totally flat backwater just does not hold many bass.

"Once you choose a backwater, you usually work it by eliminating different types of cover or depth zones, just like you do in a lake," says Velvick. "Spinnerbaits and crankbaits are two of the best

Fishing Logs In Rivers

Trees toppled into rivers are primary cover both along channels and in backwater areas. River bass and baitfish use fallen trees as hideouts and as shields from the current.

"In a river, the best trees lie in eddies that are next to the current," explains pro angler David Wharton. "The current washes baitfish into these calm areas, and the bass hide in the treetops to ambush them. This pattern is especially good in summer and fall."

For fishing fallen trees in rivers, Wharton uses spinnerbaits, buzzbaits, jigs and worms. Also, he's especially alert for the presence of baitfish.

"If I pull up to a tree and throw in a spinnerbait, and I start flushing shad with that bait, I feel like I'm fixing to catch some fish," he says. "I think that's one thing you really need to look for."

Arkansas pro Larry Nixon says most rivers have off-colored water, so the bass normally hang in shallower trees than in reservoirs. Also, fallen trees exposed to current tend to have fewer branches than laydowns in calm areas.

"Usually you'll have a lot of logs and maybe three or four short, stumpy arms with all the limbs gone, so you're working closer to the main trunk," Nixon says, adding that when fallen trees are exposed to current, bass normally hold on the downcurrent side of the trunks.

He suggests making several casts to a tree.

"You may have to work a trunk four or five minutes to get the right cast or the right lure. Maybe they won't hit a spinnerbait; they want a worm. Other times they don't want a worm. They want a crankbait banging around in there, something more erratic. It's a process of elimination until you find out what they want."

backwater lure choices, because you can retrieve them quickly to cover the water."

"Sometimes you fish a backwater by keying on something completely different from its surroundings," adds Cook. "In spring, for example, I like to locate a hard bottom that the bass will use for spawning. The amount and type of cover, the availability of food and even the depth nearby may not be as important as a place to spawn."

Oxbows, those small, crescent shaped lakes formed when silt gradually forces a river to change course (the Mississippi River is famous for its oxbows), can be considered a type of backwater, even though many actually have a complete flow-through of water from the main river. The Mississippi's Tunica Cutoff, west of Memphis, is probably one of the best-known oxbows in the South, and with good reason, as it annually produces excellent bass fishing. Tunica offers abundant cover, good depth changes and excellent water quality.

"Oxbow lakes vary greatly in both size and quality," cautions Velvick, "and this is probably a situation in which local information can be your best guide. Getting into or out of an oxbow often depends on the river's water level, and low water can make them inaccessible."

On some rivers, the very back of a tributary creek can be a backwater of sorts. The Potomac River's Mattawoman Creek, for example, is filled with lily pads, laydown timber and other cover; current is not a factor, and the channel itself provides a nice depth change. Each autumn the creek produces a surprising number of bass, and has given up at least one bass over 10 pounds to a shocking-boat crew from the Maryland Department of Natural Resources.

Rivers occasionally present two of the very same problems as lakes, which are: rapidly rising water and muddy water. Like lake fishing, both can drastically change fishing techniques.

"For rapidly rising water, bass still tend to move to the newly flooded areas, just as they do on lakes," says Cook, "but many of these places are simply too shallow for a boat.

"Instead, look for steeper banks where the bass can't go any farther. The best banks will have some shallow water and freshly flooded grass and bushes, but the steep bank stops the bass from getting out of reach. In places like this, pitching a plastic grub or tube to the bank and slowly swimming it out will frequently catch these bass.

"In muddy water, you may have to go downstream and perhaps even into the tributaries to find clear water," the former biologist notes. "Muddy water is the same in rivers or lakes in that it really stops bass activity. I've run 20 and 30 miles down a river to get ahead of muddy water and find catchable bass."

Overall, says Velvick, knowing how to fish big rivers properly is an integral part of bass fishing today. In fact, rivers sometimes can be easier to fish than big lakes. Simply search the current for bass in summer and winter and the backwaters in spring and fall, he advises, and you'll be well on your way to taming even the mightiest of waterways.

BASSING THE BACKWATERS

To these river fishing experts, heavenly hot spots are found off the main channel — the more remote, the better

JUST GETTING THERE can be half the battle in fishing the backwaters of our nation's rivers. Kansas pro Brent Chapman once drove a 17-foot aluminum boat through 300 yards of tangled stumps, twisted laydowns and thick hyacinths to access a bass fishing hot spot in Louisiana's Red River.

The gamble was worth it, rewarding Chapman with a lucrative second place finish.

"If you're willing to risk going a little farther and putting a few more scratches on your boat, you are going to catch more fish," says Chapman.

"You can figure out an oxbow a lot quicker than you can a 30,000-acre lake because the fish are more condensed," says the Kansas pro. "Then you take what you learned on that backwater and apply it to other backwaters on the same river."

And to other backwaters on other rivers during other tournaments.

The pros' successes should serve as incentive for anglers to venture into uncharted waters, too, whether they are fishing the James River in Virginia, the Pearl River in Mississippi, or the Osage River in Missouri.

Chapman believes that cover may vary, with Florida backwaters, for instance, featuring cypress trees instead of oaks, and tidal rivers offering grassy shorelines instead of laydowns.

"But fish seem to set up in the same types of areas. Just diagnose the types of baits to use in the water you are fishing," he suggests.

In addition to being consistent in where they will be, backwater bass see relatively less fishing pressure, meaning they often will be easier to catch.

"I got so many bites back in there that I didn't even go back out the last day of practice," Chapman recalls of his victory in the backwaters of the Red River.

First of all, though, how do you find these backwaters?

"Your best bet is to hire a pilot to fly you over the river," says Chapman. "If I go back to the Red River, that's what I will do. I know there are some areas that haven't been fished."

FLIPPING and pitching is an effective technique for working irregular features in backwaters, and a jig is a productive tool for catching the fish.

Other options include talking to local anglers, as the Kansas pro did, and obtaining topographical maps and aerial photos.

Once you've targeted an area, you probably will want to take a buddy and a second boat when you venture in. It might take two of you to clean away the debris and pull you off a log if you get stuck. Don't forget a push pole, and be prepared to wade.

If you've done your homework well, once you're past the silt, the laydowns, the overhanging branches and the dense vegetation, you likely will find yourself in open water.

A flat, open area, with little or no current penetration from the river, is essentially a lake, notes Arkansas tournament angler Eddie Lindley, who spends most of his time on the Arkansas and White rivers. A "slough," or "bayou," he adds, is narrower, with two steep banks.

Rivers develop natural "oxbow" lakes when their channels alter — usually in the wake of a historic flood — and an expanse of water is left yards or even miles away from the new flow. Sometimes a shallow creek will reconnect an oxbow to a river.

Lakes typically are clearer, Lindley says, while a slough likely will have mud banks and stained water.

"I like the lakes better," the Arkansas veteran says.

Bass in sloughs are likely to be right along the bank or, if standing timber is present, at the bases of the trees.

"The best fishing is when they're right off the bank, in about 2 to 5 feet of water," he says,

INCONSPICUOUS tiny openings off a main lake or river can open up to huge backwater areas that are less pressured and hold high potential for producing big catches.

adding that his favorite bait for these fish is a Mizmo tube threaded onto a jighead.

"I throw it to the bank and let it fall to the bottom by the base of a tree. A lot of these fish feed on crawfish, and that's what this bait looks like on the bottom, with its tentacles waving. If I swim it, it looks like a bream or minnow."

Lindley and Chapman both agree that flipping jigs and tubes are among the best ways to catch backwater bass, since most times they are around woody cover of some type.

"The oxbow I fished was about a quarter-mile long originally," says Chapman, adding that he used a 1/2-ounce Lunker Lure jig. "But then when the river was dammed, the area flooded and the lake doubled in length.

"The old oxbow was 20 feet deep, and the new one was 10 feet. The best places had timber near the edges of the old oxbow. One really good spot was a tapered point where the old section met the new part. It was thick with old cedar trees, and the fish were suspended in them."

Although oxbows aren't likely to have much current except for that created by the wind, Chapman says another good place to look for backwater bass is in the outside channel bends. "If there is any current, it will stack up the baitfish there," he explains.

Windblown sides are preferable to calm areas, Chapman adds, both because the breeze will put a ripple on clear water, and it will concentrate shad and other forage fish.

The pros also agree that spring is the best time to go after bass in these remote waters. That's because the main river usually is high, muddy and cold because of upstream rains. Protected by wood, vegetation and silt, oxbows and sloughs are less impacted, and their warmer and clearer water makes them fish magnets.

"March and April are the times for real heavyweights," says Lindley, who caught an 8-pound, 6-ounce largemouth in a backwater early one spring. He likes to fish a red Rat-L-Trap once the water reaches 55 degrees. His usual strategy is to fish the lipless crankbait so it just clips the edge of a grassbed or other cover. "If I bump a stump, a bite is almost automatic," he adds.

Fall also can be a good time, as bass follow shad out of the cooling river and back into more comfortable backwaters.

If the water is deep enough, bass might stay in these areas during winter. Summer, however, usually

EDDIE LINDLEY says versatility is the key to success in fishing backwaters. He likes to flip and pitch jigs and tubes, but he also will throw crankbaits, topwaters and buzzbaits.

is the time to follow the bass out of the backwaters and into the cooler and more highly oxygenated river, the experts say.

Still, Chapman believes that if backwaters are substantial, some bass stay there year-round. "Yes, the majority will move in and out," he says. "But some bass will homestead and spawn there. The fish that are born there will stay and grow into mature fish there."

Whether the fish are residents or just visiting, their positioning and inclination to feed will be affected by water level fluctuations. While backwaters aren't influenced much by mainstream currents, they do rise and fall with the rivers to which they are connected.

"Fish follow the rising water," Chapman says. "If the rise is slow and consistent, the fish will bite just fine. You'll just have to look for them farther back in the bushes."

A really fast rise, he adds, will cause only a few bass to follow the new water level; the rest will stay near their old ambush areas for a while and then eventually move to the new banks.

"With falling water, fish will stay along the edges as long as they can," he says. "They know that baitfish congregate along the banks."

Chapman prefers steady or falling water for fishing backwaters, as does Lindley.

"A rise will kill a bite quicker than a drop," the Arkansas angler says. "When it's falling, the fish are more object oriented. With the rise, they spread out and are harder to find."

Chapman cautions that anglers who venture into backwaters should remember that fluctuating water can affect more than just the bite. "Fish know more than we do," he says. "If the water is falling, they can quickly disappear. But if you go in and don't pay attention, you might not have enough water to get out."

The best backwater, Chapman says, is as disconnected as possible from the main river, but still accessible. "That's what I found on the Red River," he says. "The fishermen who were out on the main river had to make drastic changes in their patterns because of what was happening out on the river, but I could remain there in the backwater and not have to worry about that."

Still, what seems to be the perfect backwater bass haven can be subject to change. "You might not be affected by rains and runoff up the river," Chapman says. "But if you get a local rain, it's going to affect the bite. You might want to abandon that backwater for a while and give the fish a chance to adjust."

Most times though, backwaters are a good bet for catching more and bigger bass — if, like Chapman and Lindley, you don't mind going a little farther and putting a few more scratches on your boat.

BACKWATER BASS will sometimes feed aggressively along the edges of aquatic plants.

DEAD TIDE TACTICS

When you can't go with the flow in tidewater fisheries, you can still coax bites between tidal changes

D URING A KEY TOURNAMENT on the tidal Potomac River, BASS millionaire angler Denny Brauer hit pay dirt in a small, nondescript tributary on the Virginia shoreline north of the launch site.

Unlike many other anglers, who ran from hole to hole during the tournament, Brauer never left that little creek. He chose instead to spend more time fishing and less time running. Brauer's strat-

egy was a simple one: Why go looking for bass when you're already catching them?

Veteran tidal river bass anglers agree that the best time to put a quick limit of fish in the boat is when the water is moving. A rising or falling tide turns bass on, and anglers who can stay with that moving water can pick up good numbers of fish. While some pros have mastered the art of "running the tides"— keeping up with moving water — others, like Brauer,

DENNY BRAUER will commit and stay in one area on a dead tide. While there, he will fish everything he can until the tide changes.

have learned how to fish their way through the stages of the tides. Even the tough stages.

"I learned that if I try to run the tides to stay on moving water, I just get burned," says Brauer. "Since I started fishing through the stages of the tides in one area, my success has increased dramatically. The fish change as the tides change, and if you can alter your presentation, you don't need to constantly look for moving water."

Woo Daves, arguably the best tidal water bass angler in the country, would much rather look for moving water, but he's often forced to fish through the dead stages of the tides. The 2000 Bassmaster Classic winner also took a second, third and fifth place in the three world championships held on the James River.

"If you don't know the water very well and if you aren't real good at reading tide tables, it often pays to stay in one area and pick it apart," says the Virginia resident. "If you try running on an unfamiliar tidal river, you might end up stuck on a mud flat for six or eight hours."

Daves admits that catching lots of bass on a slack tide is a tough proposition, but as Brauer demonstrated once on the Potomac, a tournament angler doesn't need many bites.

Dean Rojas, a western pro who now competes in BASS events held nationwide, has fished for bass in tidal waters on both coasts.

"My favorite time to fish is during the last few hours of a falling tide. I think that's true of most professional bass anglers," says Rojas. "That's when the fish are actively feeding, and I can catch good numbers of bass."

But even he is sometimes forced to fish those few hours when the seagulls sit idly on pilings, and bass and baitfish call a temporary truce. Life in and around a tidal river seems to come to a grinding halt when the water stops moving.

Weather, a ticking clock or heavy fishing pressure can force Rojas or any tidal bass angler to stay put in an area, even if he wants to search for moving water. Patient anglers, however, can follow Brauer's lead and make the best of a bad situation by adjusting their tactics. Despite all you've heard — or the tough fishing you've experienced — fishing on a dead-low tide or a slack-high tide doesn't mean you'll go without a bite for an hour or more. However, you certainly will have to change your approach.

LOW TIDE

In a way, a low tide can be one of the best times to fish a tidal river. In places like the Potomac River, the water can fluctuate by about 3 feet. On California's Delta and New York's Hudson River, the tide varies by as much as 5 feet, or even more. When the tide ebbs, it leaves acres of cover high and dry, particularly in the backs of creeks, where mud flats are covered with aquatic vegetation. Fallen trees that had been flooded just a few hours back are now barely wet, and large sections of grassbeds that seemed to stretch to the horizon are too shallow to hold fish. In short, the bass have fewer places to hide, and finding suitable habitat is as easy as looking for it.

According to Daves, a dead-low tide is the time to concentrate your efforts on a few pieces of isolated cover and slow down your presentations. That's exactly what Brauer did during his Potomac River victory, and it's what Rojas likes to do when he can't look for moving water.

"I'm going to look for fallen trees and docks that stick out into the creek channel on a low tide, and I'm going to throw worms with a real light weight to the ends of those pieces of cover," says Daves. "The main thing you want to look for is the deepest structure around. The bass will stay on those all day and just move up and down with the water."

the pilings of a weather-beaten dock. Within minutes, he boated the first of seven bass that would put him in first place.

Each time the Missouri pro came to a likely piece of cover, he methodically picked it apart, flipping a tube or jig right into the ends of fallen trees, docks or sunken barges.

"When the tide is low and it isn't moving, you have to fish a piece of cover thoroughly," emphasizes Brauer. "The bass just aren't very aggressive, and they won't move far to hit a bait."

Rojas and Daves agree that bass in tidal rivers are different than their lake-bound kin. Sometimes, it takes 10 casts to the same spot to produce a strike.

"I don't really worry about fishing behind another angler in tidal water," explains Daves. "Unless the guy ahead of me is fishing each piece of cover real thoroughly, I'm confident that if I throw a different lure, I can catch fish he is going to miss. I'm going to work a piece of cover so hard that I know a fish is or isn't there when I leave."

In areas with large expanses of submerged aquatic vegetation, Rojas will move to the outside edge of the grassline and methodically drop plastic worms to points, pockets and other likely looking areas. The bass tend to pull out of the shallows and hold in the deeper water along that outside edge, he explains.

Although he will fish more slowly, Rojas typically won't leave a bait on the bottom for more than a second or two, choosing instead to put the lure in as many spots as he can.

"I'll give it two or three hops before I lift it and put it in another pocket," he adds. "During a dead-low tide, you almost have to put your bait in

A slack tide means the water isn't flowing, and that's why Daves switches to a lighter worm weight — 1/8 ounce or even 1/16 ounce. The smaller sinker allows the bait to fall slowly, an important factor when tidal bass are inactive. Although he insists on using smaller plastic worms like a 6-inch Zoom U-Tail or a 4 1/2-inch ring worm in just about all tidal water situations, the real key is to fish a piece of cover thoroughly.

"One of the nice things about fishing on either a dead-low tide or a slack-high tide is that you don't have to contend with moving water," notes Daves. "When the tide is really moving, it's hard to keep a lure in the strike zone because the current just pulls it away. You also tend to get hung up a lot more when the tide is flowing hard. On a slack tide, you can work a fallen tree or a dock much better than when the water is moving."

That's exactly what Brauer does in slack tide situations. As he entered the small creek on the Potomac during the BASS contest, he repeatedly dropped a 5-inch tube, his trademark lure, tight to front of their noses. I think that's where anglers go wrong: They move too fast and try to cover too much water."

HIGH TIDE

The problem tidewater bass anglers face when the tide reaches its full height is an overabundance of great-looking water. Aquatic vegetation, fallen trees, and riprap shorelines that were dry a few hours before are now covered with enough water to hold every bass in the river. All of it looks good, leaving anglers with one question: Where do I start?

"A full high tide that isn't moving is my toughest time simply because the fish can move back into the thickest cover," says Rojas. "In many cases, you just can't get back to the fish to put a lure in front of them."

On the other hand, he adds, bass are more aggressive during a full high tide than when the water is at its lowest, so faster moving baits like spinnerbaits and buzzbaits allow him to search for those scattered bass. Other reaction baits such as Rat-L-Traps, Excalibur's Swimmin' Images, and Zoom Super Flukes can draw strikes from bass suspended over submerged vegetation.

During the Potomac tournament, an abnormally high tide flooded a large flat covered with spatterdock, allowing Brauer to move back into the cover and pull a Strike King spinnerbait over the submerged vegetation. Enough quality bass slammed his lure to keep Brauer focused on the area and the tactic.

"I don't have a favorite slack tide, although the fish certainly are more active on a full high tide," notes Brauer. "I just try to stay with the fish and adjust my tactics as the fish move up and down with the water."

Daves will push his boat as far back into the cover as he can, because that's where the bait goes, and it is where the bass are likely to be. Like Rojas and Brauer, he will switch to faster moving baits and try to draw fish out of the thick cover. Smaller baits tend to work better in tidal situations, he adds, so he favors 1/8- and 1/4-ounce spinnerbaits and buzzbaits.

Higher water also means less cover on which to get snagged. That's why topwater baits with multiple treble hooks such as Pop-Rs, Zara Spooks and Tiny Torpedoes are other great choices.

"I tend to catch better quality fish on a high tide than during any other stage of the tide," says Daves, "but you still have to make more casts to the same areas or the same piece of cover to catch fish. That's just the way tidal bass are."

A STANDING TREE provides an excellent spot at high tide, while a laydown offers great potential during the low tide. Ideally, you can fish the same area twice.

HOW TO FISH AMERICA'S BASS STREAMS

Here's a primer on how to catch bass from moving water

ACROSS AMERICA, four major kinds of "running water" exist: creeks, upland rivers, lowland rivers and tidal waterways. A good example of how some river systems metamorphose through these four stages is the New River. When the New begins in the mountains of North Carolina, it is little more than a highland creek populated by rather undersize smallmouth. By the time this stream enters Virginia, the New has become a full-blown river and the smallmouth themselves are accordingly larger.

When the New and Gauley commingle to form the Kanawha in West Virginia, the river evolves into a lowland stream; and the smallmouth become fewer in number and share the stream with spotted and largemouth bass. Largemouth bass become dominant by the time the Kanawha empties into the Ohio, which in turn unites with the Mississippi. And the largemouth in Old Muddy, before it dumps into the Gulf of Mexico, feel the tugs of tidal forces.

Each stream in this quartet is unique in its own way, and the black bass that inhabit these waters exhibit distinctive traits. Here, then, are tips on how to angle for this country's moving water bass.

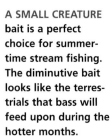

A SMALL CREATURE bait is a perfect choice for summertime stream fishing. The diminutive bait looks like the terrestrials that bass will feed upon during the hotter months.

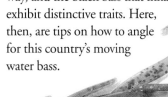

HOW TO FISH UPLAND RIVERS

West Virginia outfitter Dave Arnold comes from the school that upland river smallmouth are a breed apart.

"All species of bass are unpredictable, but river smallmouth are the most unpredictable," says Arnold. "I think this is true because the world of a river smallmouth is dominated by the rushing of water. Because a smallmouth's environment is never static, its mood is constantly changing."

Despite a river smallmouth's world being in a perpetual state of flux, Arnold relates that only three main places hold quality fish and that those locales attract fish from spring through fall.

Arnold, whose operation offers guided trips on the New River, says that the lip, or top of a rapid,

is the premier holding area. This location is where current picks up a great deal of speed before the streambed suddenly drops, in effect creating the rapid. Smallmouth move to the lip to feed, often quite aggressively.

The outfitter's second-favorite place is the bottom of the rapid where the current slows noticeably. If an eddy forms in this area, work the area where a line forms between two currents traveling at different speeds and/or different directions.

The third hot spot is what Arnold calls a mini-break in the current, which is typically just a small pocket of water behind a rock or boulder. These are the most underfished places on a river, he says, especially if the rock is submerged.

Lure choices on upland rivers are very uncom-

plicated, Arnold says. In the spring, toss tubes and crankbaits; in the summer, try buzzbaits and grubs. During the early fall, make long casts with Tiny Torpedos and Phillips Crippled Killers, as low, clear water and spooky fish are common. Later in the season, after autumn rains tint the water, tie on jig-and-pigs, spinnerbaits, grubs and crankbaits.

HOW TO FISH LOWLAND RIVERS

From his home in Oak Hill, W.Va., guide Jim Ayers frequently samples the waters of the Kanawha and Ohio — two of the better lowland rivers in the East. He says these two waterways host the three major species of black bass.

"Although you can sometimes catch smallmouth,

THE EDGES of deep pools where the current begins to pick back up again are prime areas for catching stream smallmouth.

largemouth and spots from the same place, generally you will find them in different habitat on lowland rivers," says Ayers. "For example, smallmouth are more likely to be found out in the main river channel, largemouth are more likely to be in feeder creeks or in backwaters, and spots are lucky to get the leftover places that the largemouth and smallmouth don't prefer.

Rocks in all their many forms are the predominant cover in lowland streams, adds Ayers. Riprap banks, submerged boulders and pebble and chunk rock flats all must be factored in as to where the bass may hold on any given day. Wood is a secondary form of cover, and may take the configuration of docks, tree laps, beaver lodges, brushpiles and various kinds of flood debris.

Lowland waterways are typically quite shallow. Fish often take

up station at depths of 1 foot or less, especially on summer mornings and evenings, and rarely do fish hold — or find — water that is more than 12 feet deep.

Regardless of the season, current influences where bass locate. Ayers states that smallmouth will move behind current breaks, largemouth will look for stillwater locales, and spots — although they can be found in both places — generally have to take whatever they can find.

Seasonal patterns are fairly simple. The spawn can bring some of the best fishing of the year with largemouth moving to feeder creeks, coves and marinas, while smallmouth seek out pea gravel points. Slug-Gos and finesse baits, such as tubes, are the guide's choice then.

The summer months bring the most consistent and best action on many lowland rivers. Ayers says his favorite summertime pattern is to fish a log lying vertical to a rocky bank. A buzzbait churned past the wood can bring a strike at any time of the day, but especially early and late. Texas rigged 4-inch Berkley Power worms excel when the fish move to deeper water later on a muggy day. Docks and woody debris are reliable places to seek fish.

The water often becomes extremely clear during the fall, and finesse baits are standard then. Expect the fish to group along dropoffs. If winter is late arriving, Ayers claims that good fishing can continue into late December. At this time, he exclusively fishes jigging spoons over deep dropoffs.

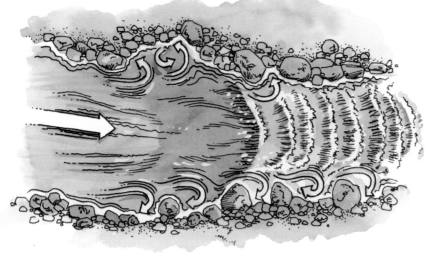

OVERHEAD VIEW OF A RAPID
The best fish zones are the top 100 feet to 200 feet above a rapid. Generally, a "pocket" of "transition water" develops in these locales. Current increases just above the rapid. Eddies above and below the rapid direct water upstream. Structure such as rocks and logs create current breaks. These current changes stir up food, thus fish. As the rapid continues downstream, "microeddies" develop all along the edge. These, even if very small, are great smallmouth zones. Fish them if you can as you head downstream with the current. This can be difficult and dangerous if you try to run the rapid and fish at the same time. The last place for excellent smallmouth fishing is the bottom of the rapid.

HOW TO FISH TIDAL RIVERS

Virginia guide Teddy Carr fishes extensively on upland rivers, tidal waterways and lakes. He is frankly in awe of tidal largemouth.

"When I think of a tidal largemouth, I think of a cover-oriented fish that is very, very aggressive — much more so than a lake largemouth," he says. "If you put a tidal largemouth and a lake largemouth in an aquarium, I have no doubt that the tidal fish would kill the one from a lake, regardless of which was bigger. The nature of a tidal bass is that of a beast."

Aquatic vegetation is an important part of the environment for any species of black bass, but is especially crucial for this cover-oriented fish, continues Carr. Spatterdock, coontail, elodea and hydrilla are favored submergent plants, while reeds and lily pads are preferred emergent varieties.

These bass also gravitate toward wood cover, and perhaps no kind of fish habitat boasts as wide a variety of wood as do tidal rivers. The wood cover along tidal rivers endures the daily ebb and flow of the tides, as well as periodic flooding. Because of this constantly changing and unstable environment, structure of any sort often does not endure. Carr lists sunken, crumbling and/or wrecked barges, piers, docks, pilings, duck blinds and old boats as examples.

Whether Carr targets vegetation or wood, a major objective of his is to find cover that has a significant dropoff (in this habitat, a foot or more) nearby. Tidal rivers are typically shallow; the term, "deep water access," often refers to areas that lie in 4 to 7 feet of water. For example, an ideal situation would be a hydrilla bed that grows in 1 to 3 feet of water and has a dropoff on one side in 4 or more feet.

Seasonal patterns are often quite different from those on impoundments. For instance, Carr says that the spring period is often the worst time to fish a tidal river, given the fact that heavy rains and snowmelt upstream can result in cold, muddy water that can delay the season for weeks. Once the spring does finally arrive, Carr likes to work emerging vegetation with 1/4- to 3/8-ounce spinnerbaits with Colorado and willowleaf blades and chartreuse-and-white skirts. During the spawn, floating worms and jerkbaits come to the fore as the fish move to flats in just a few feet of water.

The summer months, especially the dog days, are Carr's favorite times to visit tidal rivers. He often begins the day with 1/4-ounce buzzbaits, Rebel Pop-Rs and Norman ZZ Tops. Later in the day, crankbaits such as Norman MNs and Bomber Model 2As, both in fire tiger, are productive. Four-inch V&M ringworms in chameleon and in black/chartreuse tail are also good.

The fish remain aggressive well into the fall, continues the guide, with logjams and eddies being particularly good areas to prospect. Carr's No. 1 bait then is a 3/8-ounce jig tipped with a V&M V-chunk. Many years, the fine sport endures into the winter months (again, unlike the fishing on many lakes) with dropoffs and the jig-and-pig pattern pre-eminent.

How To Fish Creeks

Blane Chocklett guides for smallmouth on the James and New rivers and he also takes clients to trout streams — a type of fishing he feels makes him a better small stream bass angler.

"Going after creek smallmouth is more similar to fishing for mountain trout than it is fishing for lake largemouth," says Chocklett. "The feeding lies for the smallmouth and trout are very similar.

"For example, both will be in places where they expend the least amount of energy to gain the greatest amount of food. A good example of this type of place is where two currents traveling at different speeds merge."

Trout and smallmouth foods in this environment are also very similar. Both species will forage on such prey as sculpin, black-nosed dace, creek chubs, hellgrammites and stoneflies. Various aquatic hatches, especially those of the mayfly family, are important food sources as well.

Classic creek smallmouth holding areas include riffles, runs, plunge pools, eddies, grassbeds and logjams. The absolute best place to fish on a small stream is the tail end of a pool, Chocklett says. Look for the biggest smallmouth to move into these areas during low light conditions.

Seasonal patterns are rather uncomplicated. In the spring, when the water temperature is in the 40s and 50s, the Virginian works crawfish and baitfish imitations slow and deep. Later in the spring, minnow imitations and 1/4-ounce crankbaits, such as Big Os, are productive choices. Summer fishing finds Tiny Torpedos, 1/4-ounce buzzbaits and plastic worms and crawfish to be effective. And in fall, the hair jig-and-pig returns to the scene.

INDEX